# Dharma Messages on the Amida-kyo

John Iwohara

Copyright © 2011 John Iwohara

All rights reserved.

ISBN:0984823204
ISBN-13:9780984823208

# DEDICATION

To All my friends in Dharma:
Thank you for constantly reminding me just how rich life can be.

# CONTENTS

|   | Preface | iii |
|---|---|---|
| 1 | Introduction to the Amida-kyo | 1 |
| 2 | Section One | 5 |
| 3 | Section Two | 9 |
| 4 | Section Three | 15 |
| 5 | Section Four | 22 |
| 6 | Section Five | 28 |
| 7 | Section Six | 35 |
| 8 | Section Seven | 38 |
| 9 | Section Eight | 41 |

### Appendix

| 1 | People of the Amida-kyo | 51 |
|---|---|---|
| 2 | The Jetavana Garden | 57 |
| 3 | Notes on Romanization | 61 |
| 4 | Notes on the Text | 63 |

# PREFACE

*Dharma Messages on the Amida-kyo* was written with Dharma School teachers and parents of Dharma School children in mind. It is hoped that by helping adults to introduce the Amida-kyo to a younger audience that it will help them to have a greater understanding of the tradition they are a part of. Through sharing the timeless history of the Sutra it is also hoped that the reader will gain a greater appreciation for the meaning and richness of life that the Sutra tries to reveal.

The content of this book is based on a series of Dharma School messages given at the Seattle Betsuin beginning during the 2000-2001 school year and concluding during the 2001-2002 school year, from materials used in study classes on the Sutra, and messages given during the morning services at the Venice Hongwanji. During the Sunday morning services at the Seattle Betsuin the Dharma School students, their parents, and their teachers all chanted sections of the Amida-kyo. Following the chanting a message was given based on what was chanted during the service.

In publishing this book I am indebted to the Seattle Betsuin Dharma School and the Venice Hongwanji for allowing me the opportunity to develop these materials and for allowing me to use these materials during their services. A special thank you must go out to the Dharma School students themselves (ranging in age from two months to ten years old) for learning how to chant the Amida-kyo and then for being so enthusiastic in listening to the messages given. I only hope that I have been able to impart to them some of the wonder and beauty of the Nembutsu that the Amida-kyo tries to show us. I am also indebted to all the daily morning service attendees of the Venice Hongwanji. It was their daily attendance that gave me the courage to make this work public.

In publishing this work I also need to give my thanks to Reverend Kazunori Abe, Kevin Tanemura, Gail Kaminishi, Alan Groves, Thomas Hoshino and Sean Iwohara for reading early drafts of the manuscript, for their suggestions and their comments.

Finally, I would also like to give my thanks to all the teachers of the Nembutsu I have been able to meet and to express my indebtedness to them. If these teachers did not share their time and wisdom with me, this current publication would not be possible. It is almost entirely due to their patience and work that I have been able to gain any kind of understanding and appreciation for the depth and beauty of the Nembutsu tradition that I am so freely allowed to participate in.

This presentation of the Amida-kyo borrows from the traditional style of Sutra analysis. Although I wish I could have presented a more doctrinal study of the Sutra, this current presentation of the Amida-kyo lacks the analysis and depth to do the Sutra justice. I have only been able to present some of the "hidden" truths that can be found within the Amida-kyo. From this presentation, however, if even a single Dharma School student is motivated to further study the Sutra that generations have worked to preserve and present to them, then I hope I am allowed the conceit of considering this work, limited as it is, a success.

# 1 INTRODUCTION TO THE AMIDA-KYO

Although the Sutra are those writings that record the spoken words of a Buddha, it can also be understood as a distinct literary form with its own conventions and structures. Because of this, many of the early studies of the Sutra included a literary analysis of the structure of the text. This method of study is known as *"kadan wo kiru"* or "Outlining the Sutra." In this outline, the Sutra is understood to be divided into three large sections. These sections are known as the *Jobun* or Introductory Section, the *Shoushuubun* (lit. "True Essence Section") or the main body of the text, and the *Ruzuubun* (lit. "Flowing Transmission Section") or the section that discusses how the Sutra is to be transmitted to later generations.

These major divisions are also divided into smaller subsections. The *Jobun*, for example, is divided into two subsections or the *Shoushinjo* (lit. "Introduction Indicating Faith") and the *Hokkijo* (lit. "Introduction of Arising"). The *Shoushinjo*, which lets us know why the Sutra should be considered authentic, is also referred to as the *Tsuujo* (lit. "Common Introduction") because the contents of this section of the Sutra is common to all Sutra. In contrast to this the *Hokkijo* explains the reasons for the Buddha to begin his message that would eventually be recorded as the Sutra. It is also referred to as the *Betsujo* (lit. "Separate Introduction") because the contents of this section are unique to each of the different Sutra.

The *Shoushuubun* is typically divided into several subsections. These subsections indicate how the reader has outlined the contents of the Sutra. The different sections found in this particular presentation of the Amida-kyo have tried to outline the Sutra into its logical partitions while trying to keep each section about the same length for chanting purposes. For example, Section One includes the *Shoushinjo* and the initial section of the *Shoushuubun*. Because of this, the outline created is sometimes forced, but hopefully still allows the reader to get a sense of the Amida-kyo from the traditional literary analysis style of Sutra studies.

The *Ruzuubun* is the concluding section of the Sutra. The chief function of the *Ruzuubun* is to indicate who is responsible for transmitting the message to future generations. This section also helps us to appreciate the importance of sharing what was received. Part of what is received from the Amida-kyo is an appreciation of the living legacy of Buddhist transmission that we have become active participants in. In the transmission of the Sutra, which is also done through our participation in the chanting of the Sutra, we hear about those whom first heard the Sutra. Moreover, we now sit in their seats.

We are told how the story begins in India; we are told about the original audience that is comprised of people whose names are in Sanskrit. The Sutra was then translated into Chinese and in passing the teaching onto a Chinese speaking audience the Chinese applied their literary analysis of the Sutra to help outline the contents of the Sutra and ensure its proper transmission. As the Sutra was transmitted to Japan the Japanese adopted the Chinese characters or *Kanji* and began to chant the Sutra in their pronunciation of the Chinese.

After its transmission into Japan, the Sutra was explicitly identified by the Japanese monk Honen Shonin[1] as one of the three major Sutra that define the Pure Land Buddhist Path. This understanding was passed onto Shinran Shonin, the founder of the Jodo Shinshu[2] school of Buddhism. Jodo Shinshu would become the first organized school of Buddhism to cross the Pacific Ocean and helped to introduce Buddhism and the Amida-kyo to North America and the English speaking world. Our chanting the Sutra and our trying to understand the text—our participation today as those who are now listening to the Sutra just like the very first audience did in India—becomes part of the history of the Sutra: a text that has been able to reach us by transcending (through embracing) the different languages of Sanskrit, Chinese, Japanese, and English.

The Sutra on the Buddha's explanation of Amida Buddha.

Commissioned Translation (During the era of) Youshin,[3] by the Tripitaka Master[4] Kumarajiva

In this way I have heard. At one time, the Buddha was at the country of Sravasti's Jetavana Garden together with the great monks numbering 1,250 people. They were all great Arhat known amongst the peoples. The aged Sariputra, Mahamaudgalyayana, Mahakasyapa, Mahakatyayana, Mahakausthila, Revata, Suddhipanthaka, Nanda, Ananda, Rahula, Gavampati, Pindolabharadvaja, Kalodayin, Mahakapphina, Vakkula, and Aniruddha were present. These and other great disciples together with the various Bodhisattva and Mahasattva like the Dharma Lord Initiate Manjusri, the Bodhisattva Ajita, the Bodhisattva Gandhahastin, and the Bodhisattva Nityodyukta were present. These and other great Bodhisattva together with the various heavenly deity rulers, and the great assembly from the immeasurable (number of) various heavens were present. At that time the Buddha spoke to the elder Sariputra. From here in the westward direction, past ten-ten thousand-one hundred million (10,000,000,000,000) Buddha lands there is a world called Sukhavati (Utmost Bliss). In that land there is a Buddha with the title Amida. The Buddha is now currently explaining the Dharma.

# 2 SECTION ONE

In Section One of the Amida-kyo we are given an explanation as to why the Amida-kyo is true. We are given a time ("At one time"), a place ("the Jetavana Garden[5] in the country of Sravasti"), and a person ("I") or Ananda who is explaining what he has heard the Buddha say. We are also given a list of people who was there listening to this message given by the Buddha. It is a list of 1,250 people[6] together with various Bodhisattva,[7] Mahasattva,[8] heavenly deity rulers, and heavenly beings from the uncountable number of heavens. Although we may wonder why the Sutra makes a point to list so many different names,[9] we discover that in our daily lives we tend to do the same thing. For example, if we are unsure about going to see a new movie or attending some social function like a party, we typically ask our friends if they have seen the movie or ask who is going to the party. We respect the opinion of our peers or those whom we feel are knowledgeable about certain things. The more people that we respect who attend these functions the more confidence we have about our own participation. Our parents know this is true as well. That is why when we are not sure about going somewhere our parents are always sure to tell us about any of our friends who might be attending. In the Amida-kyo we are told about all these wonderful people and beings who took the time to listen to the Amida-kyo. I am sure it was Ananda's hope, as well as the Buddha's, that if we heard about all these people listening to this particular message that we too would take the time to listen.

Reading the Sutra, which also includes chanting the Sutra, is not just about reading the words of the text. As we chant the Amida-kyo we are able to hear the words of the Buddha ourselves. When we sit and gather to listen to the Amida-kyo while chanting it, we discover that the Amida-kyo is not just some message that was given over a thousand years ago. We discover that right here, right now we have been allowed to recreate the drama that became the Amida-kyo. We all know for a fact that *at one time, here at the temple, I have heard.* We discover that "The Buddha is now currently explaining the Dharma."

If the Amida-kyo was being written today, then it would be our names listed in the Sutra. Beginning the Sutra by taking the time to list the people in attendance is one way to show us how important every person is. The Sutra does not simply say, "a large group of people gathered" and make us feel that the Sutra is important only because a large crowd gathered. Instead, it was because individuals gathered to hear the message that the Amida-kyo becomes important.

Although the list does not mention all 1,250 people in attendance, we are nonetheless being told how important each and every person is. Because of this the Sutra helps us to discover how important each and every one of *us* is. Shakamuni Buddha had to tell us about the Vow of Amida Buddha. It is a vow that promises to save each and every one of us. Although it is a vow meant for all of us, the Vow—like the Sutra—is not important because of how many people it can save. Instead, it is important because it is meant specifically for me. I am not one person out of many. I am not "hey you." I am a distinct person who can be called by name. It is this very unique person, this distinct individual that Amida Buddha has vowed to save. It is this truth that this section of the Amida-kyo is trying to help us to see. We are, in other words, being helped to see how important each and every single person is. In particular the Sutra is helping us to see the truth of how important *my* life is.

Section One, however, also includes something unique to the Amida-kyo. As mentioned in the Introduction to the Amida-kyo the Introductory Section of the Sutra typically has a well defined *Betsujo* or section that describes the circumstances surrounding the Buddha's giving of his message. In the Amida-kyo we are simply told that the Buddha just began speaking to Sariputra. Because of this, the Amida-kyo also became known as the *"mumon jisetsu kyo"* or "the Sutra that was explained by (Shakamuni Buddha) himself without being questioned." Because this is unique to the Amida-kyo many great thinkers began to ask, "Why would Shakamuni Buddha just begin talking to Sariputra?" Of the Buddha's many disciples Sariputra was known as the "disciple most wise."[10] One of the answers that is given to answer this question is the Amida-kyo is the lesson that Shakamuni Buddha most wanted everyone to hear. Because of this, the Amida-kyo continues to have great importance and is one of the most read Sutra today.[11]

Section One ends by telling us that Amida Buddha and His Land is very, very far away from us. It is ten-ten thousand-one hundred million or 10,000,000,000,000 Buddha Lands away from us. 10,000,000,000,000 is a huge number. For some perspective let us assume that a Buddha Land is 1 mm (about 0.04 inches) in size. 10,000,000,000,000 Buddha Lands would still be 10,000,000 km (about 6,213,699 miles) away. The average distance from the Earth to the Moon (the semi-major axis) is 384,403 km (238,857 miles). You could take 13 round trips between the Earth and the Moon and you still would not have traveled a distance far enough to reach Amida Buddha's Land. Of course, a Buddha Land is probably much larger than just 1 mm.

Despite this great distance from us, however, Amida Buddha is still trying to share the Dharma with each and every one of us and through this sharing help us to achieve the same Great Awakening, the same Great Enlightenment as the Buddha's.

*Sariputra, for what reason is His Land titled and called Utmost Bliss? The multitudinous beings of that land do not have the various sufferings; they only receive the various pleasures. Thus, it is titled Utmost Bliss. Again, Sariputra, in the country and land of Utmost Bliss there are seven layers of railings, seven layers of nets, and seven layers of rowed trees. All these have the four jewels and surround and encompass the land. For this reason his country is titled and called Utmost Bliss. Again Sariputra, in the country and land of Utmost Bliss are the lakes of the seven jewels; the waters of eight virtues fill the inside of the lakes. The lake beds are of pure gold sand that is strewn across the earth. The four banks have stair-like paths of amalgamate gold, silver, beryl, and crystal. Above are the palaces. These again have gold, silver, beryl, crystal, white coral, red pearl, and agate adorning the palaces. The lotus blossoms in the lakes are large like chariot wheels. The blue colored ones give off a blue light, the yellow colored ones a yellow light, the red colored ones a red light, the white colored ones a white light; their pure incense (fragrance) is light and wondrous. Sariputra, in this country and land of Utmost Bliss, these adornments of virtue are realized.*

# 3 SECTION TWO

In this section of the Amida-kyo we find part of the explanation as to why the Buddha's Land is called *Sukhavati* or "Utmost Bliss." This section begins with a description of the people who reside in the Buddha's Pure Land.[12] We are told that they do not have the various sufferings and that they only receive the various pleasures. Although we are not told specifically what these pleasures are, the rest of the Sutra is meant to help us understand how it is possible to find a place that is free of strife and is filled with joy. The explanation begins with a description of seven layers of railings, nets and trees. It is described as a very orderly and beautiful world. Nothing comes as a surprise; everything is just as it should be.

In contrast, we sometimes describe our world as "chaotic." This is a source of great distress for many of us. However, despite sometimes feeling that our world is chaotic it is much more orderly than we sometimes want to acknowledge. If the world were truly chaotic then there would be no point in studying or learning. We could neither share nor love in a chaotic world. In a chaotic world we would neither know if tomorrow follows today, nor would we know if today follows yesterday.

It is because there is order, because there is truth that we can appreciate how special and not random something like "today" or "my life" is. It is because of this truth that we can begin to talk about a path. We begin to learn how important actions are and how important the heart that we have is. We can begin to appreciate the causes and conditions that surround my life and not take these things for granted. We can also learn how not to blame everything on someone or something else. We learn that our world is much more orderly and beautiful than we may have originally imagined. We are helped to understand this truth because the Pure Land, as a land of Enlightenment itself, acts like a mirror that helps us to see the truth and beauty found in our world beneath the chaos that we sometimes create for ourselves.

To help us understand that the Pure Land of Amida Buddha is a land of Enlightenment itself we are told of the seven rows of railings, nets and trees. These three kinds of seven rows help us to understand the Enlightened essence of the Pure Land, its truth, because seven is a number that lies beyond the number six or the number of suffering realms that Enlightenment has to overcome.[13] The Sutra also helps reveal to us that the Pure Land has been a world of Enlightenment throughout the three time periods of past, present and future.

Of the three elements that encompass the Buddha's Pure Land the final object we are told of is the seven layers of trees. Trees are very important in Buddhism. In the description of the historical Buddha's life there is almost always a tree involved. For example, the Buddha was born at the foot of the Asoka tree, the Buddha became enlightened under the Pippala tree (later to become known as the Bodhi tree), and the Buddha died between the twin Sala trees. Trees, then, have nurtured and protected the Buddha. In a similar way, trees nurture and protect the Pure Land of Amida Buddha. Because it is a land of Enlightenment itself it is also a land that guarantees *my* Enlightenment.

To help us see how the Pure Land is a land that can help me to become a Buddha, the number seven is again repeated in describing the number of lakes inside the Pure Land. These lakes are said to be filled with water that has the eight virtues.[14] Water is very important. Because our body is roughly 60% water, water is something we require just to survive. Water, however, is not just a source of life it can also be the source of a well-lived life. Water is used not just to nourish the body, but also to cleanse the body. We are reminded, for example, of the story where Prince Siddhartha gave up his ascetic practices in order to search for the way of the Middle-Path.

Before seeking this path the Prince bathed in the waters of the Neranjara River as a means to cleanse his spirit and abandon his attachment to the ascetic practices that became a burden to him.

Likewise, the water in the Pure Land is the source of a deep spiritual life. It is the water that allows us to cleanse ourselves from our burdens, our attachments, and allows us to recognize our potential as a future Buddha. From this perspective the eight virtues that the waters of the Pure Land are said to have takes on added significance. In the very first sermon given by the historical Shakamuni[15] Buddha —the turning of the Wheel of Dharma—eight is given as the number of virtues we must perfect in order to achieve Enlightenment. This is known as the Eightfold Path of Buddhism.[16] The Dharma, which can be symbolized by the water, becomes both the source of our lives and that which allows us to cleanse ourselves of our false attachments that cause us to suffer. It is, in other words, the source of a well-lived life: the life that finds its ultimate expression as Buddha-hood.

Section Two also talks about the ground cover of the Pure Land. Instead of dirt, the land is made of gold sand. Sparkling jewels can also be found everywhere instead of the rocks that we find in our world. This description of the Pure Land is one way to make us want to go to the Pure Land. It is only natural that we would want to be born in a land of such beauty and riches. However, this description of the Pure Land is not simply meant to talk about a beautiful world that is in our future, but to help us understand our own world in the present. For example, if we were to find ourselves in a world like the Pure Land what would we do? There is gold sand scattered everywhere and atop of this sand are countless numbers of sparkling jewels. If we could bring back even some of these things with us we would be rich beyond our wildest dreams. Because of this we would probably collect as much of the sand and rocks of this land as we possibly could. If we did these things how would the people of *that* land view us? To help answer this question let us imagine a person who came to our land and started to pick up all the dirt and rocks. Would we look at this person as being strange? Why would, we might ask, someone work so hard to collect things that are found everywhere? We might even laugh at the stranger who was collecting the dirt and rocks, "Why collect all this worthless stuff?" The question the Pure Land makes us ask is, "Is this stuff really worthless?" Although it is true that dirt and rocks can be found everywhere, that does not mean that these things are worthless. Without things like the dirt and rocks, the common stuff, our world would not exist at all. From this perspective, things like dirt and rocks are as precious as gold sand and jewels. The Pure Land helps us to see this truth.

Next, within the lakes we are told that there are large lotus blossoms that are blue, yellow, red, and white in color. Lotus blossoms are frequently depicted as the Buddha's seat of Enlightenment. It is for this reason that the Buddha's statue is almost always standing or seated on a lotus blossom. Although the water of the lakes found in the Pure Land is made of crystal clear water, the lotus is typically found in murky waters. Found floating above the murky water the petals of the lotus blossom—despite being found in that environment—are not dirtied by the water. This image helped people to understand the nature of a Buddha who, despite being surrounded by the passions of greed, anger and stupidity,[17] is not sullied by these things; the Enlightenment of the Buddha remains pure.

The different colors of the lotus blossoms help us to consider that we do not have to be identical. For example, we do not have to wear the same style of clothing, listen to the same music, or even have the same color skin. In the Pure Land these differences are not despised but are accepted as part of the beauty that defines the Pure Land. Furthermore, despite these differences, each lotus blossom is able to share in each others' light. Similarly, our world also has many differences. Everyone at the temple is not the same age, and not the same height. Some of us do not even have the same number of teeth. It is because we can gather right here, right now that a temple becomes possible. It is also because we can gather—despite our differences—that the temple becomes a wonderful experience. Everyone adds something unique and special to the temple. We may be different, but it is because we share the same water of Enlightenment that we are able to appreciate and respect these differences: instead of becoming something that can divide us, these differences help us to see the beauty of the life that we are now able to share.

For example, imagine how hard it would be for us if our hands looked exactly like our feet. It is because things like our hands and feet are different that our body is able to do the many wonderful things that it is able to do. We do not think too much about these differences because we are able to see our body as a whole and not made up of distinct parts. Likewise, if we could see ourselves as a temple then it does not matter so much if everyone is not the same age, is not the same height, does not have the same color skin, or does not have the same number of teeth.

If we were to see our world as a garden, although it is beautiful to see rows and rows of the same kind of flower, it is also a thing of beauty to be able to see all the differences we may have as part of the same garden. Each flower shares with each other flower. We would be a garden with blue flowers, yellow flowers, red flowers, and white flowers. Every flower is important because every flower helps to make our garden a special garden.

Earlier I mentioned that the Pure Land is not chaotic and is orderly and beautiful. If we consider the different colors of the flowers in the Pure Land we will discover that the colors red, yellow and blue were not chosen at random: these are the primary colors. If we add white to these primary colors, the color of the fourth lotus blossom, then not only are we able to create every color but we are also able to create every shade as well. These different colors help us to see how we can do so many more things when we are able to accept and share our differences. For example, it does not matter how hard blue tries on its own it will never be able to create green, purple or powder blue. Yellow, red and white, respectively, are needed. On the other hand, when all of the colors are able to work together, every color now becomes a possibility. In a similar way, our world is also a world that depends on many different things working together. An adult, for example, cannot become a parent without a child; a person cannot become a teacher without a student. Because the lotus blossoms of the Pure Land are able to share their colors in harmony as equals, we are able to see the full potential and the utmost beauty of the garden. In sharing their lights with each other we are allowed to see every color and every shade of the rainbow reflecting off the pure water of the lakes of the Pure Land. Sharing our lives, even with something like chanting the Amida-kyo, can help us to see our world as a place filled with the beauty and vibrancy of life. The temple becomes a place where we can discover how sharing the Buddha and the Dharma with each other allows all of us, together, to become a Sangha and collectively become the three treasures of Buddhism.

Again Sariputra, this Buddha country and land is always creating heavenly music. The land is of yellow gold. The Mandarava blossoms of heaven sprinkle down during the six time periods of the day and night. The multitudinous beings of that country, at the gentle dawn, each holding flower baskets, gather the different wondrous flowers and give offerings to the ten-ten thousand-hundred million (10,000,000,000,000) Buddha of the other directions. That is, within the eating period they return and reach the home country (of Amida) to eat and drink, and (then) walk to settle the mind. Sariputra, in the country and land of Utmost Bliss there are these kinds of fulfilled virtuous adornments. Again, continuing, Sariputra, in his country there are always the various marvelous birds of mixed colors: the white crane, the peacock, the parrot, the Sarika, the Kalavinka, and the Gumyou. These various birds, throughout the six time periods of the day and night give rise to the exquisite harmonious sound. These voices softly teach the Dharma of the Five Root (Essences), the Five Powers, the Seven Attributes to Reach Enlightenment, the Eight Attributes of the Right Path and others. The multitudinous beings of that land, after hearing these voices think of the Buddha, think of the Dharma and think of the Sangha. Sariputra you should not think that these birds are really of the birth of wrongful recompense. Why is this? It is because in this Buddha country and land there are none of the three evil destinations. Sariputra, there is not even the name of the three evil paths in that Buddha country and land; how can it exist in reality? These various birds—this is all due to the desire of Amida Buddha to announce the Dharma sound—are manifested.

# 4 SECTION THREE

In this section of the Amida-kyo we are told that heavenly music is always playing in this land of yellow gold. We are also told that the Mandarava[18] blossoms of heaven are sprinkled throughout the six time periods. These six time periods divide the 24 hours of the day into time periods known as *jinjou* (lit. "early morning"), *nicchuu* (lit. "middle of the day"), *nichimotsu* (lit. "sinking of the day"), *shoya* (lit. "beginning of night"), *chuuya* (lit. "middle of the night"), and *goya* (lit. "end of the night"). These "gifts from the heavens" that are sprinkled throughout the day are gathered and then shared with all the different Buddha throughout the entire universe. These Mandarava blossoms are said to be so exquisite that simply looking upon them is able to fill your heart with joy. What does it mean for the Pure Land of Amida Buddha to be filled with these petals that fall from the sky? For one thing we know that all the beings of Amida Buddha's Pure Land wake to a gentle dawn each morning. Because of these flowers we are also told that every morning and every night is filled with joy. These flower blossoms are then gathered and shared with all the different Buddha. The joy of Enlightenment, we are told, is never meant to be kept for one's self. It is something that wants to be shared. In this sharing, however, we discover that by meeting with Amida Buddha in his Pure Land we are also able to meet with all Buddha. Furthermore, we discover that in praising the virtues of Amida Buddha we also praise all the Buddha. After sharing[19] these gifts of the Pure Land of Amida with all the Buddha, the multitudinous beings[20] then return to Amida Buddha's land to eat, drink and walk.

In this part of the Amida-kyo we are given a glimpse into the lifestyle of monks that is still practiced in many parts of the Buddhist world. Monks are required to eat their one meal of the day before the noon hour. This meal is comprised of the alms received by the monk after going out to the community to receive support. After returning and finishing their meal, monks then spent the rest of the day meditating or doing other practice. Although this section helps to create a bridge between our world and the Buddha's, the Amida-kyo does not simply tell us of a world that is distant from ours and is in our future. Instead, it also helps us to see our world in the present. Like all bridges, they can be crossed from either end. From our end, this bridge points us towards the Pure Land and helps us to see the world of Amida Buddha. It is a bridge that helps us to see that up ahead is a world of beauty and peace. From the other direction, however, we receive the Buddha's Wisdom that helps us to appreciate our lives and the world we live in.

Everything in the Pure Land of Amida Buddha is designed to help us see Enlightenment. It is for this reason that Shinran Shonin describes the Pure Land of Amida Buddha as the world of Light or Wisdom. The Pure Land *shows us* the working or activity of Enlightenment. Through this we discover the freedom found in sharing the truth and how our daily activities, including those activities that keep us alive—like eating and drinking—can be appreciated as activities that allow us to continue to share the truth that we are constantly participating in. Appreciating the beauty of the Pure Land allows us to discover our own hearts opening up and living life that is both an expression of my own joy—the life of gratitude—and a life that can help others to discover the same joy.

Following this description we are told of the birds that can be found in the Pure Land. These birds are described as being of mixed colors and include the white crane, the peacock, the parrot, the Sarika, the Kalavinka, and the Gumyou bird. Although these birds are described as being very colorful and thus suggesting how beautiful they are, the very next line states that their voices give rise to an exquisite and harmonious sound. The white crane and the peacock are known especially for their exquisite beauty, the parrot and Sarika are said to be birds that can mimic the human voice, and the Kalavinka[21] and Gumyou are birds known especially for their beautiful voices.

The Gumyou is a special bird. The name Gumyou literally means "shared life." This bird is called the Gumyou because it is a bird that has two heads but only one body. The following story is associated with the Gumyou.

One day, all the different birds who heard the voice of the Gumyou praised the Gumyou for its beautiful voice. One bird, however, inadvertently asked, "I wonder which of the two heads has the better voice?" All the other birds began to ask the same question and so it was decided that they would have a singing contest to see which of the two heads had the more beautiful voice. The two heads began to practice. The first head felt that it had a good practice session and was very confident. The second head began to worry. "Although I believe I have the better singing voice, the other head does have a beautiful voice. My voice seemed a little weak today and if I make a single mistake the other head will mistakenly be regarded as the head with the better voice. What can I do?"

In its worry the second head conceived of a way that would ensure its victory in the upcoming contest. Its solution was to poison the other head. After all, without the other head there would be no question as to who had the more beautiful voice. With this plan in mind the second head waited until the first head went to sleep, poisoned the first head's food, and then went to sleep. The next morning, after the two heads awoke, the second head waited until the first head finished its breakfast. The first head looked towards the second head and wondered why the second head was suddenly so confident given how nervous it looked the other day. "Good luck" the first head said to the second head. The second head thought, "Luck won't have anything to do with it." Unfortunately, before the contest began, the poison took effect and because the two heads shared the same body instead of simply killing the single head the entire bird was poisoned to death.

The story of the Gumyou shows us what a life lived with the three poisons of greed, anger, and stupidity will become. It is a way of life that, in the long run, benefits no one. This story, when we listen to it, helps to reveal to us the silly heart of a human being. We often find ourselves doing the exact same thing as the Gumyou bird but are not able to see it because, like the second head, we are too busy being right or too busy protecting our egos to see how our actions are harming not only others but ourselves as well. For example, although we know that war is bad, no one goes to war thinking that they are wrong. Although everyone goes to war believing that they are justified, the only thing that war guarantees is death and destruction. This is something that few, if any, could want.

The voices of these birds are said to teach the Five Root Essences, the Five Powers, the Seven Attributes to Reach Enlightenment, and the Eight Attributes of the Right Path. The Five Root Essences are those characteristics that can give rise to the Right Path. These are faith, perseverance, mindfulness, determination, and wisdom. The Five Powers are what is gained from the Five Root Essences. The Five Powers give one the strength to break free from evil. The Seven Attributes to Reach Enlightenment are mindfulness, selecting the Dharma, perseverance, joy, a heart that is carefree and assured, determination, and a heart that can discard. The Eight Attributes of the Right Path are holding right view, thought, speech, action, livelihood, perseverance, mindfulness, and settlement.[22] Learning about these qualities can help one to achieve Enlightenment. Because of this, the Amida-kyo says, one naturally begins to think of the Buddha, the Dharma, and the Sangha.

Regarding the birds that are said to be found in the Pure Land we are cautioned about how to understand their existence there. These birds are said not to be of the birth of wrongful recompense. The term "wrongful recompense" is used to describe the condition created from actions that are taken by individuals who do not have an understanding of the truth a Buddha becomes awakened to. The conditions that are created in this way, through acts that are created from the state of ignorance, can only lead to situations where suffering is the result. The Gumyou bird found in the Pure Land would not, for example, worry about which head had the prettier voice and would be fully aware of the life the two heads share together. Thus, because the birth of these birds is not due to wrongful recompense their birth does not result in the suffering known as old age, sickness, and death.[23]

We are given two reasons why this is true. The first is because the three evil destinations do not exist in the Pure Land. The three evil destinations are placed in contrast to the three good destinations.[24] Although these destinations taken together as a group describes the six realms of suffering, they are divided into "evil" and "good" destinations to describe the relative amounts of evil and good acts that were necessary to be born into these realms. The evil destinations are comprised of the realms of hell, hungry ghost, and animal. These three realms are so distant from the Pure Land that it does not even exist as a word or as a concept.

The second reason given is that these birds were manifested by Amida Buddha to announce the Dharma sound. Although this point will be made again in the sections that follow, everything in the Pure Land is there to help make clear or manifest the Dharma. Put in a different way, everything—every object or every *form* found in the Pure Land—is there to reveal the *essence* of the Dharma. The essence of the Dharma gives rise to and is revealed in the form of the Pure Land.

For example, during our services we always burn incense or do *oshoko*. We do *oshoko* not to create smoke but to help us understand the truth that the Dharma is trying to reveal to us. The act of burning incense is a ritual act that reminds us to purify our hearts and minds to be able to receive *truth as it is* and not how we want to hear it. Part of the truth that we need to *hear as it is* is the fact that if you are born you will die. This truth is revealed to us by the fact that once the incense stick starts to burn its "death" or becoming ash is guaranteed. The only way to prevent the incense stick from becoming ash is to not burn it. However, if the incense stick is never burned, it will never be able to "live" as an incense stick. Furthermore, just because the incense stick does become ash after it is burned does not mean that the incense stick disappears as if it never existed. For example, the fragrance of the incense stick, carried by the smoke of the incense, permeates the *hondo*[25] we all share. When we leave the *hondo* our hair and our clothes will still retain the smell of the incense. The incense continues to share its life with us in this way. Its life is also shared in the incense burner. The ash found in the incense burner is the collection of all the incense that has been burned there. Every new stick of incense that is burned helps to make the foundation of ash that helps the next stick of incense to burn. If we see these lessons through the form of incense burning, then we will understand the essence of the ritual or the reason why we burn incense. Through this, hopefully, we are also able to discover that no life is lived in vain. Each life helps and adds to the next. It is these truths that the Pure Land reveals to all who dwell or hope to dwell there. As a final comment to this section, because Shakamuni Buddha taught us about the Pure Land of Amida Buddha we discover how his life continues to inform our lives. Shakamuni Buddha continues to enrich and deepen our lives today. Because he shared the truth of Amida Buddha with all those gathered, because all those who followed helped to preserve this Sutra to the present day we are allowed to hear the truth that can be found in the Sutra. When we do we become part of the great transmission and are now able to help others to hear and discover the truth found in the Amida-kyo. In this sharing not only will our lives not vanish, but our lives will become a life that can help others to discover just how rich their lives are. In this way, even after death, our lives become part of the great voice that announces the Dharma sound to all.

*Sariputra, in this Buddha country and land a delicate wind does blow, and upon the movement of the various rowed trees of various jewels and the jeweled nets, a delicate and wondrous sound is made. It is as if a hundred thousand layers of instruments all played together at the same time. Those who hear this sound all naturally give rise to the heart that thinks of the Buddha, thinks of the Dharma, and thinks of the Sangha. Sariputra, in that Buddha country and land these various adornments of virtue are fulfilled. Sariputra, what should you hold in your heart? For what reason is this Buddha titled Amida? Sariputra, this Buddha's light is immeasurable, and in shining on the countries of the ten directions, there is nothing that can obstruct it. For this reason, given a title, he is called Amida. Again, Sariputra, the lifespan of this Buddha as well as the people (of this Land) is an immeasurable, unreachable asogi-kalpa. Because of this (she[26]) is named Amida. Sariputra, upon Amida Buddha becoming a Buddha from this moment ten kalpa have passed. Again, Sariputra, this Buddha has immeasurable and unreachable disciples who hear the voice (and become Enlightened). They are all Arhat and (their numbers) cannot be known through calculation. The various Bodhisattva are again the same. Sariputra, in this Buddha country and land these various adornments of virtue are fulfilled.*

# 5 SECTION FOUR

Here again we are given a description of the trees. This time, however, we are told of how when the wind blows through the trees it produces a delicate and wondrous sound. What is a delicate sound? To answer this question I will need you to close your eyes and do the following. With your eyes closed, gently blow onto your finger tips. Listen. This is what I think a delicate sound is. It is the sound that is so gentle that you cannot simply rely on your ears to hear it. You have to hear this sound with your entire body and your heart. You have to hear this sound with everything that is you. It is the sound that gently caresses you; it is the sound that you hear when the wind gently blows across the cheeks of your face. It is the sound that is like the humming voice of a mother holding onto her baby and rocking it gently to sleep. It is the sound that is like the quietly rising smoke of incense and the wondrous fragrance it brings with it. It is the sound of comfort. It is the sound of absolute assurance. This sound that you will hear in the Pure Land is of such beauty that when you hear it you cannot help but to think of the Buddha, the Dharma, and the Sangha. On the other hand, this sound that reminds you of the Buddha, the Dharma, and the Sangha is also a powerful and wondrous sound that is likened to a hundred thousand layers of instruments all playing together at the same time.

Where might we hear such a sound? Obviously it is in the Pure Land. However, even before we go to the Pure Land we can hear a very similar sound when we chant the Amida-kyo or other Sutra together. When we share our voices this is also like a hundred thousand layers of instruments all playing together at the same time. When everyone is chanting together you can hear the sound with your body, your heart and not just with your ears. When we chant we are hearing the words of a Buddha. As we chant and as we hear we are able to help others to hear and to chant these words. This unity or "oneness" that we can experience through chanting is one of the things that make the temple a special place. It makes the temple beautiful. Adornments or decorations are not just things that you can see with your eyes. When you see a beautiful flower, for example, your next impulse is to smell the flower. The smell of the flower also helps to make the flower beautiful. The adornments of the Pure Land include things we can see, things that we can touch, things that we can smell, and things that we can hear. The next part of the Amida-kyo tells us that part of the adornments of the Pure Land include things we can become.[27]

Before describing what it is that we can become, a description of Amida Buddha is given. This description of Amida Buddha is divided into the description of the Buddha's Light and the Buddha's Life. In describing the Buddha's Light the Amida-kyo tells us that the light shines on the countries of the ten directions. The ten directions are east, southeast, south, southwest, west, northwest, north, northeast, down and up. This is one of the expressions used to mean "everywhere." Because of the directions of down and up Amida Buddha's Light fills three-dimensional space. Because there is nothing that can obstruct this light the Buddha is titled Amida.[28]

Why do you suppose that Amida Buddha became the Buddha of Immeasurable Light? To answer this question we need to first consider what the nature of light is. Light is something that allows us to see things that we could not see before. For example, one night I forgot something downstairs. I knew exactly where I forgot the object I was looking for and so I decided to go down and get it. Because I have a general idea where everything is I thought that I did not need to bother turning the lights on. As I was walking, because I did not know that my wife had rearranged some of the furniture, I banged into the coffee table. When my shin hit the table it felt like it was going to explode. I felt like screaming out in pain, but because everyone was already asleep I suppressed my shouts. In creating the bruise on my shin the coffee table was instantly and miraculously transformed into a "stupid table." If I had turned the lights on and saw the table it would not have become the "stupid table." It would simply be a coffee table. This is how being able to see things clearly changes not only how much we can see, but how we see things. There are many things in our lives that we can bump into. Some of the more painful things we can bump into include old age, sickness, and death. If we are not able to see these things clearly then when we bump into these things they become "terrible and tragic." These experiences can become something that can completely ruin our lives. If, however, we can see our lives clearly, then even these things cannot overwhelm us: old age, sickness, and death are parts of our life that we can accept and even learn to appreciate. In shining upon the countries of the ten directions the light of the Buddha allows us to embrace all aspects of our life.

In learning to appreciate all aspects of our life we gain a deeper regard for Amida Buddha becoming the Buddha of Immeasurable Life. In trying to get us to understand how important our lives really are, in all of its stages, Amida Buddha has promised to embrace us wherever (space, as expressed by light) and whenever (time, as expressed by life) we may be. For example, if you are like me then when you hear expressions like, "My how big you've grown" or "I remember you when you were still a little baby" you become a little annoyed. The reason I become annoyed is because I am no longer the little child or the baby the other person keeps trying to see me as. Being greeted this way I am sometimes made to feel that the other person is not appreciating who I am in the present. I sometimes want to say, "I am not the little baby who poops in their diaper anymore." However, when you grow older, if you have children of your own, you begin to appreciate these words more and more. No, I may no longer be the baby who poops in their diaper, but that baby is still a part of who I am. I became the adult I am today partly because of all the things my parents did for me that, among other things, includes all the diaper changes.

These things, like diaper changes, may be things of our past, but they help us to appreciate the present that we are now experiencing. In the next part of this section of the Amida-kyo Shakamuni Buddha informs us that Amida Buddha became a Buddha ten kalpa ago. A kalpa is a very long time. One way that the length of time a kalpa is calculated is described in the following way. A kalpa is the amount of time it would take a heavenly being to completely wear away a stone that is 40 *li* in height, width, and depth[29] by brushing the stone once every hundred years with their delicate sleeve. Needless to say, this will take a very long time.

Why was it important for Shakamuni Buddha to tell us how long ago Amida Buddha became a Buddha? It may be something we by nature might be curious about, but it also tells us about the compassionate nature of the Buddha. As mentioned above, understanding our past helps us to appreciate the present. For example, was our birthday the very first time that our parents began to think or worry about us? The answer is more than likely no. Even before we were born our parents were constantly thinking about us. They were thinking about things like our diets and what mother should or should not eat; they were thinking about how much exercise we were getting and whether or not mother was getting enough rest; they probably also worried about what we were listening to, whether there was too much noise, and whether the type of music helped mother to relax. They were also thinking about things like what our names might be and where we would live. Our parents did all of these things for us before we were born or when we begin to measure how long we have been alive. In a similar way, we discover that the Pure Land of Amida Buddha, with all of its wonderful adornments and all of its lessons, was prepared for us since before we can imagine.

Our religious awakening often begins with the question, "Who am I?" In answering this question we also discover who or what we can become. Although all religions express hope in what our lives can become, the various religions express perhaps similar but different ways of seeing this potential of human life. How does the Amida-kyo express this potential of our lives? Before the Sutra begins to help us answer the question "Who am I?" it is important to remember that the Sutra begins by first telling us about the Pure Land and then talks about Amida Buddha. This is important because we are not only given an image of the Hero, but through this discussion of the Pure Land and Amida Buddha we are also being helped to discover that we already have everything we need to answer the questions "Who am I?" and "What can I become?" In helping us to first understand "Who I am" the Sutra tries to show us what our lives really are: it is a precious and rare treasure. The Amida-kyo reminds us that "It is difficult to receive a human form; now, I have already received (it). It is difficult to hear the Buddha-Dharma; now, I am already hearing (it)."[30] It is from this understanding that we begin to realize the full potential and meaning of our lives. My life in the Nembutsu—the life that is nurtured within the Wisdom and Compassion of Amida Buddha—is a life that helps me to see that I am also a part of countless other lives throughout the broad expanse of time. There has never been a moment when my life was not affirmed in this way. For example, even if I were to find myself all alone, Immeasurable Life still adorns the life that I live. My life is not possible without the support of others. Likewise, the life that I live helps to complete Immeasurable Life. Without my life, even if it is just one out of billions, Immeasurable Life would not be possible. My birth has within it all these various meanings. That I am able to meet with the Buddha-Dharma, the teaching of a Buddha, also demonstrates how my life is made possible only through the help of others. Simultaneously, however, my receiving these gifts also gives meaning to the activity of the other.

The Pure Land and Amida Buddha helps us to see that the adornments or decorations of the Pure Land are not just things. It is also found in the immeasurable quality of life itself. In Shinran Shonin's understanding of why there is a Buddha and His Land he states, "It was for me and me alone."[31] The immeasurable quality of life is found in the people and beings of the Pure Land. To help us to answer the questions of "Who am I?" and "What can I become?" the Amida-kyo helps us to see that people are also a very important adornment of Amida Buddha's Pure Land. Amida Buddha became a Buddha and is helping us to become a Buddha by allowing us to see how people make the Pure Land beautiful. We are also helped to see how people adorn my life, and how my life is part of that beauty. This is also part of the message of the Amida-kyo.

*Again, Sariputra, the multitudinous beings born in the country land of Utmost Bliss are all Avaivartika, and within these are many who will become (a Buddha) in one lifetime; these are extremely great in number and this cannot be known through calculation. It can only be explained in an immeasurable, unreachable (number) of asogi-kalpa. Sariputra, those multitudinous beings who hear and give rise to vows should desire to born in that country. Why is this? This is because they can gain (the ability) to meet together in one place with the various superior and good people. Sariputra, with (just) the causes and conditions (created by) slight roots of good and the bestowing of virtues of happiness one cannot gain birth in this country. Sariputra, if there is a good man or good woman, and if (he or she) hears the explanation by Amida and holds the Name and Title (of Amida) even if it is for one day, even if it is for two days, even if it is for three days, even if it is for four days, even if it is for five days, even if it is for six days, even if it is for seven days, then with a heart that is single and one not disturbed that person, in anticipating the moment of life's end, will have Amida Buddha together with the various sages appear before (him or her). This person, at the time of their end, (their) heart does not waver, and they thus gain the birth of going to Amida Buddha's country and land of Utmost Bliss. Sariputra, my seeing this benefit is the reason for my explaining with these words. If there are multitudinous beings who hear this explanation, they should give rise to vows and be born in this country and land.*

# 6 SECTION FIVE

The goal of every school of Buddhism is to achieve Buddha-hood or to become awakened by the truth. This aspect of the Buddha-Dharma is made clear in the first sentence of Section Five that states that there are "many who will become (a Buddha) in one lifetime." The path towards Buddha-hood is, however, a difficult one. There are many obstacles along the way. Any of these obstacles can lead one astray from the straight path towards Enlightenment. Going astray from the path was seen as headed in the opposite direction of Enlightenment. Because of this, becoming a Buddha seemed an impossible goal to reach. To help motivate people to continue along the path, the Buddha also talked about the status of Avaivartika. Avaivartika is the status or quality of a person who is assured that they will eventually become a Buddha. When Buddhism entered into China, the Chinese translated the term as *futaiten* which means "without back tracking." The Avaivartika, then, is someone who does not have to worry about heading in the wrong direction and moving away from the path towards Enlightenment. Knowing that you do not have to worry about "going back" is very important.

For example, one of the most difficult things to do is to quit smoking. Because of this it is better never to start. There are many things to help motivate somebody to quit smoking. The cigarette packages, for example, have labels that warn you of the dangers of smoking that include but are not limited to heart disease and lung cancer. Other studies have also shown that cigarette smoke—known as second hand smoke—is also harmful. Study after study tends to indicate that cigarette smoking, even indirectly, is a contributing factor to an early death. Because of this common knowledge, there should be no lack in motivation to quit smoking. That there is no lack in motivation can also be seen in how helping people to quit smoking has become a multimillion dollar industry. Although you can probably spend thousands of dollars to stop smoking, even after you quit there is always the fear that you might "go back" to smoking. Because of this there is the joke that goes, "I can quite smoking anytime. I've done it lots of times." If all the time and money you spend to quit smoking simply results in going back to smoking at a later time, then there really does not seem to be a reason to try to quit. This logic makes it difficult for some people to even try to quit smoking. If, however, there is a method that absolutely guarantees that a smoker can quit and never has to worry about going back to smoking, then anyone and probably everyone who is interested in quitting smoking will want to try that method.

In this example, smoking represents the un-enlightened state of human existence. There are many reasons why we would want to leave this state, but if there is no guarantee that we can then we may conclude "why bother?" and continue to smoke even when we know that it is not the best thing for us to do. In order for us to not reach this conclusion, the Buddha has told us of a stage where we do not have to worry about returning to the world of suffering, or in our example the world of smoking. It is for this reason that Buddhism places such importance in becoming an Avaivartika, or the state of "non-retrogression."

However, it is not enough to know that you do not have to worry about going back to smoking. You have to actually quit in order to gain any benefit from trying to quit. It is for this reason that the Amida-kyo also takes the time to tell us that those who will become Buddha are more numerous than we can count. From this explanation found in the Amida-kyo we discover how Pure Land Buddhism is a path founded to help people achieve Buddha-hood.

The next line of the Amida-kyo continues with this description of Amida Buddha and the Pure Land as a path towards Buddha-hood. This time, however, we are given the reason why anyone would want to be born into the Pure Land. It is described as a place where we can meet the various superior and good people all in one place just by holding the Name and Title of Amida Buddha. Holding the Name and Title of Amida Buddha or *Namo Amida Butsu* is also called the Nembutsu.[32] How can we know that this place exists beyond believing or having "faith" in the words of a Buddha? To do this we are given a glimpse into the reality of this world whenever we gather and meet at the temple. We gather at the temple only because of the Nembutsu. It is because the world of the Nembutsu allows us to see how we are all one—regardless of how old we are, how tall we are, or whether we are a boy or a girl—that these distinctions that can separate us dissolve away. Not only do these distinctions dissolve away, but in understanding the meaning and heart of Amida Buddha, as revealed by the Nembutsu, we discover how all life supports all other life. This is the web of life that we participate in.

The Amida-kyo continues by saying that birth in the Pure Land of Amida Buddha cannot be done by small roots of virtue. Small roots of virtue refer to all the Buddhist Practice other than the Nembutsu or saying Amida Buddha's Name. What is it that makes the Nembutsu so meaningful? Although this topic continues into the next line of section five, Zendo Daishi[33] interprets "small roots of virtue" to mean "the various good acts in accordance with conditions." Shinran Shonin in his *Yuishinshomoni*[34] states:

"What is called '*accordant conditions, the various good that is the feared difficulty for birth*' is: '*accordant conditions*' are those various good (acts) that are cultivated in accordance with the various conditions of multitudinous beings that rely upon the (state of their) various hearts; these (merits) are transferred to the (land of) Utmost Bliss. This, in other words, is the Dharma gate of the 84,000 (paths). Because these are all the roots of good of Self-Power,[35] and because one despises this as not leading to birth in the Real Recompensed Land,[36] it is called '*the feared difficulty for birth*.'"[37]

The difference, then, between the Nembutsu and other practices is the difference between the heart of the Buddha and the hearts of multitudinous beings that are all at different stages of development based on their respective circumstances or "various conditions." This is why, for example, we continue to make distinctions that separate us even while we have experienced and understood the joy of what it means to share. In describing the differences between the various other practices and the Nembutsu, the Amida-kyo continues by saying that if a good man or good woman hears the explanation by Amida Buddha and holds the Name and Title (of Amida Buddha) for even one day, two days, three days, four days, five days, six days, or seven days, then Amida Buddha together with the various sages will appear before that person and that person will gain the birth of going to Amida Buddha's country and land of Utmost Bliss where we will be able to meet together with the various superior and good people.

The other practices, in contrast, those that rely on the ever changing status of the person doing the practice, will take years or lifetimes to perfect in order to be born into Amida Buddha's Land. Although this is one way to describe the superiority of the Nembutsu, it is still a strange explanation. Why, for example, does the expression not begin with seven days and then count down to one? In other words, if only one day is necessary, what is the point of doing the Nembutsu for seven days? Does the Amida-kyo only want us to do the Nembutsu for a maximum of seven days?

In emphasizing the importance of just the single day, the Amida-kyo makes clear to us that the Nembutsu is the "Easy Practice"[38] while emphasizing its superiority over other practices. For example, in the *Senjakuhongannembutsu-shu* ("Compilation on the Selected Nembutsu of the Primal Vow") written by Honen Shonin[39] are the words:

"...first there is the case of superior and inferior, second there is the case of difficult and easy. To begin, what is (called) superior and inferior is (this). The Nembutsu, this is superior. The other practices, these are inferior. What is the reason for this? The Name and Title (of Amida Buddha) is where the 10,000 virtues take refuge....Next, (in) the case of the difficult and easy, the Nembutsu is easy to cultivate, and the various practices are difficult to cultivate."[40]

In this description of the Nembutsu practice, Honen Shonin states that the Nembutsu is both the superior and easy practice. Because it is superior it will allow a person to be born into the Pure Land of Amida Buddha with just a single day of practice. This is contrasted with the other practices—the slight roots of good and the bestowing of virtues of happiness—that are insufficient in and of themselves regardless of how long they are practiced.

Given the superiority of the Nembutsu practice, one reason why the Amida-kyo does not count down from seven days is because the Nembutsu practice is described within the context of anticipating life's end. In this context, the Nembutsu practice is easy to continue until life's end. It does not matter if it is just one day because the Nembutsu is superior to all other practices. On the other hand, it is also easy enough to continue until the very last moment of life be it one day, two days, three days, four days, five days, six days, seven days, weeks, months, or even years. In this way the Nembutsu is a practice that allows us to appreciate our life in its totality. This would include all the different stages of our life including birth, old age, sickness and death.

In its emphasis on the single day, however, this passage also tells us how important certain events in our life can be. There are, for example, experiences that have changed our entire lives. These experiences may include things like meeting the person who became your best friend, meeting a wonderful teacher, becoming an older brother or sister, or experiencing the death of someone very close to you like a parent. Some experiences are so important and overwhelming that experiencing it just once, even if for one day, is enough to change our lives. The Amida-kyo makes clear that the Nembutsu is one of those experiences. In meeting with the Nembutsu, or the Great Practice selected by the Primal Vow of Amida Buddha, we can discover the meaning of "it is difficult to receive a body in human life, yet we are already receiving it; it is difficult to hear the Buddha-Dharma, yet we are already hearing it."

In sharing Enlightenment with us through the Amida-kyo, we see how Shakamuni Buddha wanted us to be able to add meeting with Amida Buddha—hearing *Namo Amida Butsu*—as one of those experiences that have changed our lives forever. It is an experience that can change us even in a single encounter. It is something that can change us in a single day, and can be a change so great that it can even transform our appreciation of the past.[41] Like Shinran Shonin before us we are helped to declare how the Vow of Amida Buddha that took five kalpa of thought, the same Vow that required aeons of practice to fulfill, and the Vow that was fulfilled ten kalpa ago was all done for my sake. Through this we hopefully learn how to appreciate the lives of our parents, grandparents, the birth and life of Shinran Shonin, the birth of Prince Siddhartha,[42] the Enlightenment of Shakamuni Buddha, and Shakamuni Buddha turning the Wheel of Dharma[43] not as things that happened outside of my life but as gifts that have helped me to hear *Namo Amida Butsu* and helped me to finally meet with my life. We are helped to discover the countless causes and conditions that make each and every day in my life possible. We are allowed to see, and thereby fully experience, the countless or immeasurable lives that help to make not just life, but my life possible. We discover the world where I am embraced and not forsaken. We live a life that allows us to say, "I am glad that I was born."

The teaching found in the Amida-kyo, the Nembutsu teaching, helps us to discover the joy of living a life that is shared in its entirety. Continuing to live this shared life is one of the promises of the Pure Land. It is here that we are allowed to gather in one place and share our lives. We discover a world where we are allowed to affirm my existence, and in so doing affirm the life of all others. Wanting us to have this gift, the Amida-kyo states, is the reason why Shakamuni Buddha taught us about the Buddha and Land of Immeasurable Life.

Sariputra, just as I am now praising the inconceivable virtues of Amida Buddha, again from the Eastern direction are Aksobhya Buddha, Meru-dhvaja Buddha, Maha-meru Buddha, Meru-prabhasa Buddha, Manjughosa Buddha and like them the various Buddha numbering (as) the sands of the Ganges each from their respective countries, take out their broad and long tongues, and inclusive of all the Three Thousand Great Thousand Worlds explain the true and real words, "All you multitudinous beings, truly (you) should have faith in the Sutra that is kept in mind and protected by all the various Buddha who praise these inconceivable virtues." Sariputra, in the worlds of the Southern direction are Candrasuryapradipa Buddha, Yasahprabha Buddha, Maharciskandha Buddha, Merupradipa Buddha, Anantavirya Buddha and like them the various Buddha numbering (as) the sands of the Ganges each from their respective countries, take out their broad and long tongues, and inclusive of all the Three Thousand Great Thousand Worlds explain the true and real words, "All you multitudinous beings, truly (you) should have faith in the Sutra that is kept in mind and protected by all the various Buddha who praise these inconceivable virtues." Sariputra, in the worlds of the Western direction are Amitayus Buddha, Amitalaksana Buddha, Amitadhvaja Buddha, Mahaprabha Buddha, Mahanirbhasa Buddha Ratnalaksanna Buddha, Suddharasmi-prabha Buddha and like them the various Buddha numbering (as) the sands of the Ganges each from their respective countries, take out their broad and long tongues, and inclusive of all the Three Thousand Great Thousand Worlds explain the true and real words, "All you multitudinous beings, truly (you) should have faith in the Sutra that is kept in mind and protected by all the various Buddha who praise these inconceivable virtues."

# 7 SECTION SIX

Section Six begins what is called the *roppoudan* or "section on the six directions." It is called this because in this section the Buddha of the six directions give praise to the inconceivable virtues of Amida Buddha. In Section Four the quality of Amida Buddha's light was described as lighting the different lands of the ten directions. Like the expression "ten directions," the expression six directions is a phrase used to mean "everywhere." The six directions are east, south, west, north, down, and up. These six directions also indicate the direction or flow of the truth. Truth was seen as being both dynamic and constant. To express this dynamic notion of the truth, truth was seen as having a direction or flow. To express the constant aspect of the truth, this flow or direction of the truth is always the same. Because of this, in describing the truth, the direction always begins in the east and turns clockwise from that direction or south, then west, to north. Because truth is also seen as that which "lifts" us, the final two directions that fill three-dimensional space is from the direction of down to up. The Buddha that praise the virtues of Amida Buddha, then, praise the truth while being part of the truth.

As part of the flow of the truth the Buddha of the six directions take out their broad and long tongues and give assurance to all the beings that occupy the *Three Thousand Great Thousand Worlds*[44] that having faith in the teaching of the Amida-kyo is reliable. The physical trait of having a broad or fat and long tongue is one of the thirty-two attributes of a Buddha. Each of these attributes becomes a physical representation of an Enlightened being. Just as human beings have developed certain attributes that have helped to make humans what they are, Buddha are also said to have developed attributes that help to identify them as Buddha. For example, one distinctive attribute of a human being that distinguishes humans from most other primates is upright bipedal motility. The ability to walk upright, together with opposable digits,[45] has allowed humans to freely use their hands and develop increasingly sophisticated tools. Being able to walk upright also gave humans a distinct survival advantage, despite not having a well-developed sense of smell, because humans were able to see farther out than a hunched over posture would allow. These traits help to define not only the characteristics but the abilities of a human being.

The thirty-two attributes of a Buddha are also seen in this light. The trait of having a broad and long tongue is used to describe how a Buddha only speaks the truth. The reason this trait has this meaning is because having a fat and long tongue would make it extremely difficult to talk. Under these circumstances one would want to talk only when it was absolutely necessary. Revealing and assuring us about the truth of the Amida-kyo is one of those times that caused all the Buddha to speak.

Although one can argue that it was probably sufficient for us to know that Shakamuni Buddha praised the virtues of Amida Buddha, the way the Amida-kyo is written firmly impresses upon us the depth of the Nembutsu or *Namo Amida Butsu*. For example, the Amida-kyo was given without anyone previously asking Shakamuni Buddha a question. In other words, Shakamuni Buddha had a need to teach us, through Sariputra, the virtues of Amida Buddha and His Land. In teaching us about the truth of the Nembutsu, the Amida-kyo takes us through the flow of the truth. While in the flow of the truth we are able to meet and are introduced to the Buddha of the six directions. In meeting these Buddha they reveal to us their broad and long tongues and assure us yet again about the truth of the Nembutsu. The virtues of Amida Buddha—the Wisdom and Compassion of the Buddha that is encapsulated in the name of the Buddha, or *Namo Amida Butsu*—reveal to us the truth that the Amida-kyo has helped to make clear in the previous five sections.

*Sariputra, in the worlds of the Northern direction are Arciskandha Buddha, Vaisvanaranirghosa Buddha, Duspradharsa Buddha, Adityasambhava Buddha, Jaliniprabha Buddha and like them the various Buddha numbering (as) the sands of the Ganges each from their respective countries, take out their broad and long tongues, and inclusive of all the Three Thousand Great Thousand Worlds explain the true and real words, "All you multitudinous beings, truly (you) should have faith in the Sutra that is kept in mind and protected by all the various Buddha who praise these inconceivable virtues." Sariputra, in the worlds of the Lower direction are Simha Buddha, Yasas Buddha, Yasahprabhasa Buddha, Dharma Buddha, Dhramadhvaja Buddha, Dharmadhara Buddha and like them the various Buddha numbering (as) the sands of the Ganges each from their respective countries, take out their broad and long tongues, and inclusive of all the Three Thousand Great Thousand Worlds explain the true and real words, "All you multitudinous beings, truly (you) should have faith in the Sutra that is kept in mind and protected by all the various Buddha who praise these inconceivable virtues." Sariputra, in the worlds of the Upper direction are Brahmaghosa Buddha, Naksatraraja Buddha, Gandhottama Buddha, Gandhaprabhasa Buddha, Maharciskandha Buddha, Ratnakusumasampuspita-gatra Buddha, Salendraraja Buddha, Ratnotpalasri Buddha, Sarvarthadarsa Buddha, Sumerukalpa Buddha and like them the various Buddha numbering (as) the sands of the Ganges each from their respective countries, take out their broad and long tongues, and inclusive of all the Three Thousand Great Thousand Worlds explain the true and real words, "All you multitudinous beings, truly (you) should have faith in the Sutra that is kept in mind and protected by all the various Buddha who praise these inconceivable virtues."*

# 8 SECTION SEVEN

Section Seven continues the discussion started in Section Six. In describing the Buddha of the six directions, the Amida-kyo states that in each of the six directions there are Buddha who number as the sands of the Ganges River. The Ganges River[46] is a river that flows through the region known as Hindustan across the Gangetic Plain. The river starts from Uttar Pradesh in the north and flows into the Bay of Bengal, a delta shared by the countries of India and Bangladesh.[47] Although the Ganges River is a relatively short river[48] by world standards, it has been seen as a holy river for the Hindus from ancient times. This coupled with the fact that the river helps to support one of the most fertile regions of the world as well as some of the world's oldest cultures and civilizations help to give us a sense of the expression "Buddha who number as the sands of the Ganges."

Although the river may not be long as far as world rivers go, the Ganges River's total drainage basin covers roughly a quarter of the Indian Territory. For this reason, the Ganges River has been and is intricately involved in helping to support life, cultures and civilizations throughout the history of the Indian continent. Given this fact, although the expression "sands of the Ganges" does tend to suggest the banks of the river, it can also probably be expanded to include the entire drainage basin or the area that the Ganges River helps to support with its life giving waters. This image helps us to see how the Buddha-Dharma was probably envisioned. The sands of the Ganges River (the entire drainage basin) has been the ground from which has arisen and supported countless lives and civilizations. These civilizations have included kingdoms such as King Asoka's in the third century B.C.E., and the Mughal Empire founded in the 16th century C.E. Similarly, Buddha who number as the sands of the Ganges can provide the foundation and footing necessary for us to continue the journey of our lives. Nourished by the waters of the Dharma, there is no fear of living our lives without it being supported and embraced by the Nembutsu.

*Sariputra, what kind of heart should you have? Why is this a Sutra that has been given the title of being kept in mind and protected by all the various Buddha? Sariputra, if there is a good man or good woman, the person who hears the Name—that which is being explained by the various Buddha—as well as the title of the Sutra, then all these various good men and good women will, by all the various Buddha, be thought of and protected together, and they will all gain the (state of) non-retrogression in the unsurpassed equal Bodhi. For this reason Sariputra, as should you all, truly receive the faith of my words and that which is explained by the various Buddha. Sariputra, if there is a person who has already given rise to vows, is giving rise to vows, or will give rise to vows, then those who desire for birth in Amida Buddha's Country—these various people—will all gain the (state of) non-retrogression in the unsurpassed equal Bodhi; within this country and land, they will either already be born, are being born, or will be born. For this reason Sariputra, the various good men and good women, if they are people with faith (they) will be born in this country and land upon giving rise to vows. Sariputra, as I am now praising the inconceivable virtues of the various Buddha, these various Buddha too are praising my inconceivable virtues with these words, "Shakamuni Buddha you have well given (rise to) the most difficult and wondrous thing; well have you within the Saha country and land, the evil world of the Five-Defilements—defilement of time, defilement of views, defilement of passions, defilement of beings, defilement of life—attained the unsurpassed and equal Bodhi, and for the purpose of those various multitudinous beings explained this Dharma that is difficult to have faith in throughout the world. Sariputra, you should truly know this. I have within the evil world of the Five-Defilements practiced this most difficult thing; (I) have gained the unsurpassed and equal Bodhi, and for the entire world have explained this Dharma difficult to have faith in. This is called most difficult. The Buddha, upon explaining and finishing this Sutra, after Sariputra and the various Bhiku, all the world's heavenly beings, human (beings), and Ashura heard that which the Buddha explained, all with joy, received faith, and departed after bowing (before the Buddha).*

*The Sutra on the Buddha's explanation of Amida Buddha.*

# 9 SECTION EIGHT

Section Eight begins with the question, "What kind of heart should you have?" Although this question is directly asked to Sariputra, this question is also meant for all those who are hearing the Amida-kyo. What kind of heart should we have? The answer to this question begins with another question or, "Why is this a Sutra that has been given the title of being kept in mind and protected by all the various Buddha?" The reason for this, of course, is the contents of the Amida-kyo. This includes the virtues of the Pure Land as expressed in the different adornments of that land, and especially through the virtues of Amida Buddha. These different virtues of the Pure Land and Amida Buddha, however, are expressed in the Buddha's Name or *Namo Amida Butsu*. Although this is also made clear in Section Four when we were first asked, "What we should hold in our hearts?" Section Eight describes how if a good man or a good woman hears the "Name" or "that which is being explained by the various Buddha" then they will be protected by the various Buddha and will gain the state of non-retrogression[49] in the unsurpassed equal Bodhi. This is the reason why we should receive the faith of the Buddha's words.

The Name or "that which is being explained by the various Buddha" is the Nembutsu or *Namo Amida Butsu*. This Sutra is kept in mind by the various Buddha because of the Nembutsu, and those who hear the Nembutsu are protected by these Buddha. Within this guardianship, one also gains the status of someone who will not "back track" from the path towards Enlightenment; the person will achieve the state of "non-retrogression." Furthermore, in following the discussion of Sections Six and Seven we are reminded once again, through *Namo Amida Butsu*, that we are embraced within the dynamic truth that enlightens a Buddha and is also the truth that a Buddha helps to reveal.

Again, within this guardianship or embrace of the truth we are led to see things correctly. For example, in correctly seeing that the objects that make up the Pure Land are adornments we are led to think of these objects more correctly. The dirt and rock of our land is not just "stuff" anymore; they become equivalent to the gold sand and jewels of the Pure Land. In thinking more correctly, we discover that our expression, our way of speaking also changes: we are better able to express our gratitude for these "simple" things that help to make my life possible. In learning how to express our gratitude we discover that it becomes easier for us to care for these things. In learning how to take better care of the things that help to make my existence possible we learn how to live our lives with more meaning: we want to live in a way that not only supports my life but also helps to preserve those things that make this life possible. Through wanting to live a more meaningful life—a life that understands the interdependent nature of existence—we discover the motivation to live a more complete life. Every moment of life becomes a gift and because of this we find ourselves trying to live the best we can each and every day. In trying to live the best we can we learn to appreciate and be mindful of where we are, and when we are. Finally, in learning to appreciate where we are, and when we are—within the truth of the Nembutsu—we discover that our hearts are constantly moving towards the direction of Enlightenment: we gain the state of non-retrogression in the unsurpassed equal Bodhi. The process just described is fundamentally the process described as the Eightfold Path.[50]

To help remember the points of the Eightfold Path—in their proper order—I use the acronym *VTSCLEMM* as a mnemonic device. *VTSCLEMM* stands for Right *View*, Right *Thought*, Right *Speech*, Right *Conduct*, Right *Livelihood*, Right *Effort*, Right *Mindfulness*, and Right *Meditation*. Although remembering the acronym *VTSCLEMM* makes it relatively easy to remember what the Eightfold Path is, Jodo Shinshu does not have to emphasize the learning of the Eightfold Path because the Nembutsu has incorporates the totality of the Eightfold Path within it. All one has to keep in mind is the Name, or *Namo Amida Butsu*.

However, just the existence of the truth as expressed through the Nembutsu is not enough. If we do not become aware of the truth or are not moved by this truth, then it would be as if the truth did not exist. We are helped to discover the truth in two different ways. First, we are helped to discover it through the Pure Land. Through the Pure Land we are helped to understand that the truth is constant: it does not move, and it cannot change. However, we may not necessarily be aware of this universal aspect of truth. The dirt and rocks of our land, for example, have always helped to support my existence. This truth does not change. If we do not become aware of this, although the dirt and rocks continue to support my life they cannot help me to understand my life despite continuing to support it: the dirt and rocks are just "stuff." In this state, although the truth lies just under our feet, we may never become awakened to it. An inaccessible truth is, for all intents and purposes, one that does not exist. Because of this, the truth is also revealed to us through Amida Buddha. Through Amida Buddha we become aware of how dynamic the truth is. We discover that Amida Buddha is always working to help us see the truth. The constant nature of Amida Buddha's work is partially revealed to us through the immeasurable life of Amida Buddha.

The work of the Buddha is to reveal to us what the truth is. From this we come to understand that a Buddha is not a "creator" in the sense of a supernatural being who is able to determine the rules or truth of the universe. A Buddha, like everyone and everything else, must participate within the truth. On the other hand, however, because a Buddha has become completely aware or awakened to the rules of the universe, the Buddha is sometimes equated with truth itself and especially to its dynamic aspect. Because of this, the Buddha is seen as a great light that fills the entire universe allowing us to see clearly. In seeing clearly we begin to appreciate another reason why Amida Buddha became the Buddha of Infinite Life: through the Buddha's teaching we discover how my life is being supported by countless other lives (including the dirt and rocks), and how my life is also a part of this totality.

This expression of how the truth works in our lives is expressed in the Primal Vow of Amida Buddha which states that if all beings do not achieve birth in the Buddha Land (and thereby achieve the same

Enlightenment), then Amida Buddha will renounce Buddha-hood: the truth must embrace all life or it will stop being the truth.

In appreciating how one is embraced in the truth it is only natural that one would want to become a full participant of the truth, or to become a Buddha. For this reason the Amida-kyo talks about giving rise to vows after receiving faith.[51] These vows, that are expressed in the past, the present, and the future, also make clear to us the activity of the truth, or how *Namo Amida Butsu* embraces us. In helping us to understand this truth, the Amida-kyo describes and allows us to participate in the process through which the truth has been revealed to us. First, we have the words of Shakamuni Buddha given through his own volition because he felt a need to share the truth that is described in the Sutra.[52] After describing the contents of the universal and dynamic nature of truth, as revealed by the Pure Land and Amida Buddha, we are then taken through the "flow" of the truth. While being taken through the flow of the truth—going through the directions of east, south, west, north, down, and up—we are also introduced to the innumerable Buddha of each direction who again praise the virtues of Amida Buddha. The truth embraces us—throughout the past, present, and future—and then motivates us to become full participants. We are moved to have faith in the truth, give rise to vows for birth in the Pure Land and through this birth to become a Buddha. As a Buddha, we will add our voices to those Buddha who praise the virtues of Amida Buddha and help to motivate others to become full participants themselves. In this way, we discover that we are both recipients and participants in the "flow" of the Nembutsu.

Following this discussion, the Amida-kyo continues by explaining that the virtues of Shakamuni Buddha—who is sharing the Dharma in our world—are also being praised by the various Buddha. This praise is especially important because our world is described as the evil world of the Five-Defilements. The Five-Defilements are listed as the defilement of time, the defilement of views, the defilement of passions, the defilement of beings, and the defilement of life.

The defilement of time is characterized by an age filled with various calamities including things like disease, pestilence, war, and famine. Unfortunately, we do not have to watch the news or read the newspaper very long to discover all of these things in our world. Despite having made many advances in medicine, for example, many diseases are still prevalent throughout parts of the world. Also, it is because our technology has made it easier for us to travel great distances over relatively short periods of time that diseases can spread much more quickly than they were able to do in the past. This same technology, unfortunately, is also something we humans constantly abuse. Because of this, we also find ourselves constantly having to protect ourselves from this technology. We find ourselves doing things like having to protect ourselves from abusing medicines to protecting ourselves from people who would deliberately transport and use diseases or other biological or biochemical agents as weapons. We have coined phrases like "mass destruction." Also in our world, despite the many peace organizations and movements that people participate in, it is still relatively rare for the world to be at peace. Paradoxically, the many peace organizations in the world today not only show us how important and necessary these organizations are but also help us to see how far away from peace we really are.

The defilement of views characterizes an age filled with erroneous views. One of the more prevalent erroneous views we are able to find in our world is the idea that life has a certain monetary value. Based on this mistaken view we discover that some people will kill other people for money. Related to this idea is the mistaken belief that the more money you have the more valuable your life is. Because of this idea, we sometimes find ourselves thinking that money gives us permission to treat somebody badly because they have less than we do. We give ourselves permission to treat others poorly because we see them as "things." The defilement of views also makes things like war possible.

The defilement of passions characterizes an age filled with the three poisons of greed, anger, and stupidity. Greed, although it is often characterized by the desire for material things, is not limited to the desire for objects. It may also include things like the desire for fame and status. Generally, greed can be defined to include all those things that one may wish for including but not limited to wanting people to behave in a manner convenient to one's self. When people do not behave the way that we want them to, we often react in frustration or anger. From this state it is not too hard for us to transform even a good friend into a despicable person or into an enemy. Doing things like this would have to be characterized as stupid: we create a world of isolation and loneliness.

The defilement of beings is characterized by an age where the quality of the being or person is of a defiled nature. This defiled nature is often characterized by the selfish personality or by the person who cannot tell the difference between right and wrong. One's conduct is based on mistaken notions such as the belief that as long as I benefit, it does not matter how it gets done: the ends justifies the means. Because of this kind of mistaken notion, actions such as killing your husband, wife or children to get money from a life insurance policy become possible.

The defilement of life is characterized by an age where one's life expectancy is shortened. In the age we live in, with all the medical advancements, we are proud of the fact that we have raised the life expectancy of a person to the 70s and 80s. We may ask ourselves, "How can this world be a world characterized by the defilement of life?" In answer to this question we discover that in our world, because it is also characterized by the defilement of time, we become so used to hearing stories about the loss of life through natural disaster or human conflict that we become desensitized to such things. With this callous indifference to life, together with living in a world also characterized by the defilement of views, we discover how relatively easy it is for us to conclude that money has more value than life. This way of viewing life can, for example, express itself in such things as concluding that it is not profitable enough to manufacture immunization vaccines and decide to stop creating the medicine. It isn't until we are able to see life as more precious than the dollar bills we print onto paper that it becomes meaningful for us to support the manufacturing of the vaccine again. In the meantime, the vicious cycle that we have created for ourselves contributes to the possible illness and in some cases even the death of a young child. Other acts such as dumping chemical waste into our environment, typically in the name of economic development, also leads to the same kind of result. These and other examples of how we are damaging our own physical and social environment abound. When we continue to damage the world in which we live in we can only expect it to effect the quality of our lives. Likewise, if we continue to damage the quality of our living space and continue to do so with abandon then this will begin to effect how long we can reasonably expect to live. These are some of the dangers found within the defilement of life.

Despite these difficulties, however, Shakamuni Buddha was able to gain Enlightenment in this world and was also able to explain the Dharma to all of us. Here we begin to see the working of the Buddha's Wisdom and Compassion. Through the Buddha's Wisdom he was able to go beyond the defilements of time, views, passions, beings, and life. In overcoming these Five-Defilements, Shakamuni Buddha was able to see and understand the world of Enlightenment as related by Amida Buddha and his Pure Land. Shakamuni Buddha's Compassion, however, is revealed to us when he taught us about Amida Buddha and his Pure Land and through this gives us a glimpse of the Enlightenment that he was able to experience and live himself. In helping us to see, the Buddha also shares his Enlightenment with all of us. Allowing us to share in the Buddha's Enlightenment, and helping us to see that we are all able to achieve or receive the same Enlightenment is the hope and vision being shared with us.

Finally, the Amida-kyo helps us to see the emphasis Buddhism places on the equality of all beings be they great or small in stature or position. This section also becomes the *Ruzuubun* for the Amida-kyo. In this concluding *Ruzuubun* section or the section where we are told who is responsible for maintaining the Sutra, we are told how the *Bhiku* or the monks, heavenly and human beings, and even Ashura[53] or warrior beings who are not satisfied unless they are fighting were all able to gather together in harmony. Especially in a world where we create, maintain and even enforce distinctions between ourselves—all things made even more powerful in a world filled with the Five-Defilements—it is often very difficult for us to find the points we have in common that will allow us to share. Even within very close families we will find skirmishes between siblings based simply on the distinction of birth order. Often, resolution comes when parents remind their children of the common bond they share as siblings versus the differences siblings emphasize in birth order.

The Amida-kyo, however, does not simply tell us that we have things in common that allow us to share. We are also given a glimpse into the potential of living a life lived as equals. We are told that this life of ours can also be the life of joy and mutual respect. Sharing this potential is how the Sutra is to be maintained. This, we are also told, is the Sutra of the Buddha's explication on Amida Buddha. This is the Nembutsu or *Namo Amida Butsu.*

# APPENDIX

# 1 PEOPLE OF THE AMIDA-KYO

The following is a list of those individuals listed in the *Jobun* section (Section One) of the Amida-kyo. The names are first given in their Sanskrit reading (minus diacritical marks) and in the Romanized reading of the names as the Sutra would be chanted as part of a Jodo Shinshu service.

**Sariputra (Sharihotsu)**
One of the top disciples of Shakamuni Buddha. He is also known as the "elder Sariputra" and as the disciple of the Buddha most wise. The Amida-kyo is directly addressed to him.

**Mahamaudgalyayana (Makamokkenren)**
One of the top disciples of Shakamuni Buddha. He is known as the disciple of the Buddha foremost in supernatural powers and is the main character found in the telling of the Ullambana Sutra. This Sutra lays the foundation for the observance of *Obon* in Japanese Buddhism.

**Mahakasyapa (Makakashou)**
One of the top disciples of Shakamuni Buddha. He is known as the disciple foremost in ascetic practices and is mentioned notably in what has come to be known as the "Flower Sermon." This sermon lays the foundation for "direct transmission" as found in Zen Buddhism. In this sermon the Buddha simply holds up a flower. Whereas all the other disciples of the Buddha were confused by this demonstration it is said that Mahakasyapa smiled or laughed in

response. Mahakasyapa is also noted in the Nirvana Sutra or the Sutra that records the final moments of Shakamuni Buddha's earthly life. It is following the Buddha's physical passing that Mahakasyapa organized and chaired what is known as the First Council of Buddhism (see also Ananda and Rahula).

**Mahakatyayana (Makakasennen)**
One of the top disciples of Shakamuni Buddha. He is known as the disciple of the Buddha foremost in explaining the Dharma.

**Mahakausthila (Makakuchira)**
One of the top disciples of Shakamuni Buddha. He is known as the disciple of the Buddha foremost in debate. He is also known as the Arhat with long nails. He promised not to cut his nails until his practice was completed.

**Revata (Rihata)**
One of the top disciples of Shakamuni Buddha. He is known as the disciple of the Buddha foremost in being calm and collected.

**Suddhipanthaka (Shurihandaka)**
One of the top disciples of Shakamuni Buddha. He is known as the disciple of the Buddha foremost in understanding.

**Nanda (Nanda)**
Half brother to Shakamuni Buddha. He originally did not want to join the Order for the love of his wife, but eventually enters the Order at the encouragement of Shakamuni Buddha. The story of his entering the Order would later be immortalized in an epic poem written in the 2nd Century C.E.

**Ananda (Ananda)**
Cousin to Shakamuni Buddha and brother to Devadatta. He is known as the disciple of the Buddha foremost in hearing (the Dharma). Ananda accompanied Shakamuni Buddha throughout his travels and was known for his incredible ability of memorization. Because of this, he played a very prominent role during the First Council together with Rahula. It was at the First Council that the doctrine of the Buddha was first compiled (see also Mahakasyapa and Rahula). Devadatta, on the other hand, becomes one of the principal "villain" characters in the *Tragedy of Rajagriha*.

**Rahula (Ragora)**
The son of Shakamuni Buddha. Rahula was born just prior to Prince Siddhartha renouncing his claim to succeed his father. Instead of ascending to the throne, the Prince abandons his family and begins his search for spiritual freedom that would eventually result in his

Enlightenment as a Buddha. Rahula is known as the disciple of the Buddha foremost in adhering to practice and is known for his diligence in maintaining the precepts. He played a prominent role in the First Council together with Ananda. It was at the First Council that the codes of conduct of a monk, the precepts, were compiled and formalized (see also Mahakasyapa and Ananda).

**Gavampati (Kyoubonhadai)**
Because it was said that his face looked like an ox he was given the nickname, "King of Oxen." He is also known as the disciple of the Buddha foremost in knowledge of the rules.

**Pindola Bharadvaja (Binzuruharada)**
Known as the disciple of the Buddha foremost in the "Lion's Roar" (ability to be heard widely or to a mass audience). He is, however, most famous for being berated by the Buddha for demonstrating the use of supernatural powers. As punishment for his acts it is said that the Buddha made him promise not to die while the True Dharma existed in this world. Although he was later forgiven by the Buddha, he became the last of the Buddha's living disciples.

**Kalodayin (Karudai)**
Known as the disciple of the Buddha foremost in teaching (the Dharma). Although his history is peppered with misconduct, he is generally described as being a very amiable person. In the end, however, when he went to try to get a couple engaged in an illicit affair to mend their ways and listen to the Dharma he was killed.

**Mahakapphina (Makakouhinna)**
Known as the disciple of the Buddha foremost in courage and dignity. Mahakapphina was born to nobility and ascended to the throne upon the death of his father. Soon after becoming King, however, he became interested in the teachings of Shakamuni Buddha. It is said that he and about a thousand of his countrymen traveled a great distance to meet with the Buddha and when they received an audience with the Buddha listened to his message. At the conclusion of the message they all entered into the order and the King renounced his throne.

**Vakkula (Hakkura)**
Known as the disciple of the Buddha foremost in health (not becoming ill), as the disciple of the Buddha with little desires, and as the disciple of the Buddha foremost in long life. It is said that he lived to the age of 160 years. However, what is most unique about his history is the fact that as a disciple of the Buddha he never gave a

message about the Buddha-Dharma to the laity. When asked about this his reply was that there were many disciples of the Buddha who were adept at giving Dharma messages and that all he was able to do was to silently enjoy the Buddha path. There is also the story of King Asoka's visit to his monument after having visited the monuments to the Buddha and disciples such as Ananda. When the King went before Vakkula's monument he asked his retainer what kind of man Vakkula was. The retainer told the King that he was known as the disciple foremost in health, with little desires, but that he also never once shared the teachings with the laity. In response to this, the King left a single coin before the monument after having made large donations to the other monuments saying, "This is enough for a person who only thinks about his liberation and does not help others." However, the caretaker of the monument quickly went to return the single coin to the King saying that Vakkula was a man of little desires and because of this wanted to return the offering. It is said that King Asoka was greatly impressed by this.

**Aniruddha (Adoroda)**
Cousin to Shakamuni Buddha. He is known as the disciple of the Buddha foremost in the Heaven's (spiritual) Eye. He was once berated by the Buddha for having fallen asleep during one of his messages. Following his scolding, Aniruddha vowed to the Buddha that he would not fall asleep even until the next day break. The Buddha responded by saying that although it is not good to be lazy, it is also not good to be reckless in ascetic practices. He again emphasized the Middle-Path. However, Aniruddha was determined to fulfill this task especially because he made it a promise before the Buddha. Ultimately, although he lost his eyesight because of his determination, he became known as the disciple who was able to open up his spiritual eye.

**Dharma Lord Initiate Manjusri (Monjushirihououji)**
"Dharma Lord" is a title that refers to a Buddha or fully Enlightened being. "Dharma Lord Initiate" is used as a title for a Bodhisattva or the person who will become a Buddha: an initiate onto the path of Buddha-hood. Manjusri is one of the two Bodhisattva that accompanies Shakamuni Buddha and represents Wisdom. In Buddhist art Manjusri is seen holding the Sword of Wisdom that can cut through ignorance with his right hand, and a blue lotus flower in his left. He is often depicted riding a lion.[54]

### Bodhisattva Ajita (Aitta Bosatsu)
Ajita is another name for Maitreya (Jpz. *Miroku*) Bodhisattva. Maitreya is prophesied to be the next Buddha in this world and is currently practicing in the Tusita heaven. Maitreya, according to the prophecy, will descend from the Tusita heaven to once again propagate the Dharma 5,670,000,000 years after Shakamuni Buddha entered into pari-nirvana.

### Bodhisattva Gandhahastin (Kendakadai Bosatsu)
Gandhahastin is a Bodhisattva that is currently said to be practicing in the Eastern Pure Land of Aksobhya Buddha. The practice of this Bodhisattva is said to center around the perfection of the Prajna Paramita or Supreme Wisdom.

### Bodhisattva Nityodyukta (Joushoujin Bosatsu)
The name Nityodyukta means "always energetic." It is perhaps an epithet for one of the two qualities that a Bodhisattva practices to perfect or Compassion.

## 2 THE JETAVANA GARDEN

The opening line to the *Heike Monogatari*, one of the world literary classics, begins, "The voice of the Bell of the Gion Monastery echoes all conditioned things are impermanent, the color of the flowers of the twin Sala tree reveals the truth that those with abundance must fade." The reference to the Gion Monastery found in the *Heike Monogatari* is the Japanese "nickname" for the Monastery established at the Jetavana Garden.

The *Heike Monogatari* was written during a period of tremendous political and social upheaval in Japan. This somber opening line also reveals how Buddhism was seen as a teaching that could help explain the social conditions of the time and as a teaching that could provide a means for a more peaceful and egalitarian society. Hope for a brighter future, a future founded on the understanding of the ultimate and equal value of human life versus a world stratified by differences in political, financial and military power, is hinted at by the reference to the Gion Monastery or the Monastery where the Amida-kyo was shared by the Buddha.

The story of the founding of the Monastery at the Jetavana Garden is shared below.

There once was a merchant named Sudatta who lived in the country of Sravasti. He was a very giving and generous man. He was especially kind to those elderly couples without children and to orphans. Because of this he was also known as *Anathapindada* or

"One who gives presents to lonely people." Hearing that the Buddha was near, he traveled to Venuvana (the Monastery of the Bamboo Forest) to hear the Buddha's message. He was so overjoyed at what he received that he went to the Buddha and asked him to also spread the Teachings to the people of his homeland. Perceiving his sincerity, the Buddha agreed to travel to Sravasti.

With this wonderful news, Sudatta immediately headed back to Sravasti to found a Monastery suitable for the Buddha and his many disciples. He thought to himself, "It should be a place not too difficult to get to, and it also must be peaceful enough for practice and contemplation." In his search he found a grove of trees (vana) that suited his needs. He immediately sought the owner of the land and found that it belonged to the son of King Prasenajit, the Crown Prince Jeta.

He immediately went to Prince Jeta and asked if he could purchase the grove from him. The Prince initially simply ignored Sudatta. Sudatta, however, was insistent and kept asking for the purchase of the grove. Prince Jeta could no longer ignore the constant requests of the old man. He refused saying with a stern and somewhat upset voice, "The land is not for sale."

This refusal, however, did not deter Sudatta. He continued to ask to purchase the land. The Prince finally gave up refusing the old man and decided on a separate strategy. He would ask for a price so outlandish that the old man would have to give up on his mission to purchase the grove from the Prince.

Sudatta asked again. This time, however, the Prince turned to the old Sudatta and finally gave him a price.

The Prince said, "Old man, I have refused to sell you the land over and over again, and yet you continue to ask me to sell you this land. It is a very important place to me and because of this it will not be offered cheap."

"I understand," replied Sudatta.

The Prince then smiled thinking that he would finally discourage Sudatta and his attempt to purchase the land.

"Very well. My price is as follows. I will sell you the land only if you can cover the entire area with gold. That amount will be my price."

Sudatta left the company of the Prince. The Prince thought, "Finally, he has given up."

The next day, however, Sudatta came back with a cart filled with gold pieces. He began carefully placing each gold piece onto the ground and began to cover up the land. He did this for each and every piece until he had emptied his cart. It did not cover much area. He left the grove again and came back with a second cart. He began placing the gold pieces down as he did with the first cart. Upon seeing this the surprised Prince asked Sudatta to stop.

"Why are you doing this, old man?" the Prince asked.

Sudatta answered by letting the Prince know that he wanted to purchase the land to give to the Buddha and his disciples.

The Prince, moved by this, said "That is enough. I will give you the rest of the land so that you can provide for the Buddha and his disciples." Delighted by this Sudatta prepared all that was necessary for the Buddha and his disciples to stay and live in the grove; the Prince had rooms built for all those who would stay at the Monastery.

In the honor of these two people who were instrumental in the founding of the Monastery, the Monastery was hence called "The grove trees of Prince Jeta, in the garden of the person who gives presents to lonely people" or *Gion* (Jeta-Garden) for short.

## 3 NOTES ON ROMANIZATION

    Romanization (transliteration of Japanese terms using the English alphabet) is based largely on the traditional Hepburn system. Certain names and terms, however, do not strictly follow the Hepburn system and Romanization based on common usage was used. Below is a list of those terms that did not follow the Hepburn system (followed by the traditional Hepburn Romanization).
    Sanskrit terms also do not include any of the diacritical marks. The names found in Section One (*Jobun* section of the Sutra) are given in Sanskrit to allow the reader to look up these names in English texts. However, the name of the historic Buddha is not rendered in its Sanskrit form (Sakyamuni) but is written as Shakamuni. Asura, one of the six realms of existence, is also rendered as Ashura. This is based on how the text would be chanted at a Jodo Shinshu service and is Romanized following the rules consistent with the traditional Hepburn system.

| | |
|---|---|
| Amida-kyo | (Amida-kyou) |
| Daimuryoju-kyo | (Daimuryouju-kyou) |
| Hoin | (Houin) |
| Hondo | (Hondou) |
| Honen | (Hounen) |
| Hongwanji | (Honganji) |
| Igyobon | (Igyoubon) |
| Jodo | (Joudo) |
| Jodo Shu | (Joudo Shuu) |
| Jujubibasharon | (Juujuubibasharon) |

| | |
|---|---|
| Kanmuryoju-kyo | (Kanmuryouju-kyou) |
| Kyo | (Kyou) |
| Myogo | (Myougou) |
| Oshoko | (Oshoukou) |
| Senjakuhongannembutsu-shu | (Senjakuhongannembutsu-shuu) |
| Shinshu | (Shinshuu) |
| Shonin | (Shounin) |
| Yuishinsho | (Yuishinshou) |
| Yuishinshomoni | (Yuishinshoumoni) |
| Zendo | (Zendou) |

Dharma Messages on the Amida-kyo

# 4 NOTES ON THE TEXT

**Introduction to the Amida-kyo**
1 Honen Shonin was the founder of the Jodo Shu (lit. "Essence of the Pure Land") school of Buddhism. It was under his tutelage that Shinran Shonin, the founder of the Jodo Shinshu school of Buddhism, was able to find spiritual peace through the Nembutsu.
2 Jodo Shinshu (lit. "True Essence of the Pure Land") is the clarification of Honen Shonin's teaching by Shinran Shonin. The Hongwanji school, which is the largest representative of the Jodo Shinshu tradition, was the first organized school to cross the Pacific Ocean. In establishing its temples throughout the West Coast and eventually reaching the East Coast of the United States, translation efforts began to present the different scriptural texts into the English language. It is my hope that this current translation can aid in helping to make this Sutra more readily accessible to the English speaking world.

**Section One**
3 The Jin Dynasty of China (265-420) is divided into two periods. The first is often referred to as the Western Jin (265-316) and the later the Eastern Jin (317-420). The period of the late Western and Eastern Jin Dynasty, because it was marked by political turmoil and ethnic divisions, was also called the Period of the Five *Hu* (roughly "ethnic groups") and Sixteen Kingdoms. During this period one of

the more influential Kingdoms, ruled by Fu Jian (符堅), was known as *Taishin*, or "The Great Qin." Later, after the defeat at the *Battle of Feishui* (Fei River), the leadership was usurped by Yao Chang (姚萇) who killed Fu Jian and established his own Kingdom using the same name. In order to distinguish these two separate Kingdoms, the former is often called "Former Qin" or "Qin of Fu" and the latter is called "Latter Qin" or "Qin of Yao." The Amida-kyo was translated during the Qin of Yao (Jpz. *Youshin*) commissioned by the 2nd generation ruler of the Kingdom or Yao Xing (姚興) and was completed in February during the year 402.

4 The *Tripitaka* or "Three Baskets" is the term used to collectively refer to the three types of Buddhist scriptures. The first is the *Sutra* or the recorded words of the Buddha, the second is the *Vinaya* or the rules of conduct, and the third basket is the *Sastra* or the commentaries. The *Tripitaka*, then, refers to the entire collection of Buddhist scriptures. The title "Master" refers to someone who is seen as an "expert" not only in the knowledge of the texts, but as someone who also serves as the living example of what it means to live according to that knowledge. It is a title given to someone who is deemed worthy of following.

5 The passage, "*Gi Ju Ki Kou Doku On*" (lit. "The tree of *Gi*, the garden of the person *Kou*") is found in the Amida-kyo. This is the full name for the Jetavana Garden. Often, however, only the first and last character or "*Gion*" is used. More information about the founding of this very famous and important Buddhist garden is found in the appendix, "The Jetavana Garden."

6 These 1,250 people were all great Arhat (Jpz. *Arakan*). An Arhat is the ultimate state of someone who has achieved the Enlightenment of the *Sravaka* (Jpz. *Shoumon*) or someone who was able to achieve Enlightenment through hearing the teachings of a Buddha. These individuals have been able to liberate themselves from the passions that are the source of suffering, and are regarded as those worthy of receiving offerings.

7 A Bodhisattva is someone who is working to become Enlightened. In Mahayana Buddhism, the definition of Bodhisattva came to refer to someone who has vowed not to achieve Enlightenment until all others have become Enlightened. *Sattva* is a Sanskrit word meaning "with life." A Bodhisattva, then, is a life with Bodhi or the seed of Buddha-hood

8 Mahasattva is a synonym to Bodhisattva. *Maha* is a Sanskrit word that has the meaning of "great," "many" or "superior." *Sattva* is a Sanskrit word meaning "with life." Mahasattva, then, means "a great being with life" or "superior being with life."
9 See also appendix, "People of the Amida-kyo"
10 See also appendix, "People of the Amida-kyo"
11 See also Section Eight, and in particular footnote 52.

**Section Two**
12 A Buddha Land is also called a "Pure Land." It is called a Pure Land because there are no "defilements" found in a Buddha Land. Defilements are those conditions that can cause suffering.
13 The six realms of suffering (from lowest to highest) are (1) Hell, (2) Hungry Ghost, (3) Animal, (4) Ashura, (5) Human, (6) Heaven. See also footnote 24.
14 The eight virtues as listed in the *Jouzengi* (lit., "Meaning of determined good") written by Zendo Daishi are: (1) clean and pure, (2) without a bad odor, (3) light (as in not heavy), (4) cool, (5) soft, (6) beautiful, (7) quenching, and (8) refreshing.
15 The name Shakamuni literally means "sage (muni) of the Shaka (clan)."
16 The Eightfold Path is part of the Four Noble Truths. The Four Noble Truths are (1) life is suffering, (2) the cause of suffering, (3) the end of suffering, and (4) the path to end suffering. The path to end suffering is the Eightfold Path or: (1) right views, (2) right thoughts, (3) right speech, (4) right conduct, (5) right livelihood, (6) right effort, (7) right mindfulness, (8) right meditation. The Buddha first taught that upon perfecting the Eightfold Path one would be able to achieve Enlightenment. See also footnote 22.
17 The three traits of greed, anger and stupidity are known as the three poisons.

**Section Three**
18 Mandarava are flowers that are also known as the "wondrous flowers of heaven," the "flowers that give joy to the heart," the "flowers that answer the desires of the heart," and as the "white flower." These flowers are described as heavenly flowers that have a wonderful color, a wondrous scent, and as being so pure that a person who views these flowers will feel a sense of joy in their hearts.

19 Sharing, it should be noted, is not something that can be "possessed." If there is a sense of possession the more correct term to use would be "lending." In sharing the flower (that is symbolic of the blooming of Enlightenment) there is no sense of "owning" the flower. It is something that comes freely. In this metaphor we are being shown that the truth is not owned by anyone, especially and including the Buddha. The truth can only be openly shared, and it is this attitude towards the truth that is being revealed to us in this passage.

20 Multitudinous being is the translation for *shujou*. The first character, *shu*, means "many." The second character, *jou*, means "birth" or "life." The term *shujou*, then, is a word that informs us that our lives are only possible because of many other lives, and for this reason we are referred to as a multitudinous being.

21 The Kalavinka is known as the bird with the most wondrous of voices. This voice is said to be so wondrous that, except for the voice of the Buddha, no voice can match its beauty. Because of this, it is said that a person cannot tire of hearing the Kalavinka's voice. In the Pure Land *Mandala* this bird is depicted as having the head of a human and the body of a bird.

22 The Eight Attributes are also translated as right view, thought, speech, conduct, livelihood, effort, mindfulness, and meditation. See also footnote 16.

23 The four attributes of birth, old age, sickness, and death are known as the Four Sufferings.

24 The three good destinations are the realms of the Ashura (the warrior), human, and heavenly being. See also footnote 53.

25 The *hondo* is the main hall of a temple.

**Section Four**

26 Although English grammar requires a pronoun, Chinese and Japanese grammar does not. Although the pronoun "she" was added to the translation it is not necessarily accurate to refer to Amida Buddha as being either male or female.

27 The adornments of the Pure Land as described in the Amida-kyo follows the order of the Land, the Buddha, and Bodhisattva. These are referred to as the *Sangon* or Three Significant (Attributes) of the Pure Land. According to the *Jodo Ron* ("Treatise on the Pure Land"), these Three Significant Attributes are comprised of seventeen

descriptions of the virtues of the Land, eight of the Buddha, and four of the Bodhisattva of that land.

28 Amida is comprised of the term *amita* that means "immeasurable," *ayus* which means "life," and *abha* which means "light."

29 A *li* is a unit of measure. One *li* is roughly equal to four kilometers (or about 2.5 miles).

30 This is the opening line to the *San Kie Mon* or the "Words of the Three Refuges." The three refuges, also known as the three treasures of Buddhism, are Buddha (an Enlightened person), Dharma (the content and source of Enlightenment. It also refers to the teaching of a Buddha), and Sangha (the collective of those who seek to become a Buddha through the Dharma).

31 The full quotation is, "As I carefully consider the Vow that took five kalpa of contemplation, I realize that it was for this single individual or Shinran." This quotation is found in the work titled the *Tannisho*. The *Tannisho* is generally considered to have been written by Shinran Shonin's disciple Yuienbo and records the words of Shinran Shonin as received by him. The title can be loosely translated, "Record in Lament of Differences" and is a work written lamenting the discrepancies found in the understanding of the teachings found within the followers of Shinran Shonin that grew following his death.

**Section Five**

32 "Name and Title" is the translation for Myogo and refers specifically to *Namo Amida Butsu*. Nembutsu literally means "Mindful of the Buddha." In Pure Land Buddhism being mindful of the Buddha ("holding the Name and Title") is expressed as the voiced utterance of Amida Buddha's Name and Title. Because of this, *Myogo* and Nembutsu are sometimes used interchangeably.

33 Zendo Daishi is one of the Seven Masters of Jodo Shinshu Buddhism. *Daishi* is an honorific title that means "Great Teacher."

34 The *Yuishinshomoni* is a work written by Shinran Shonins as a commentary to the *Yuishinsho* written by Seikaku Hoin. Seikaku Hoin was one of Honen Shonin's chief disciples. The *Yuishinsho* or "Passages on Faith Alone" is a text that describes how faith (*shinjin*) is the central theme of the exclusive cultivation of the Nembutsu. *Hoin* is an honorific title that means "Mark of the Dharma."

35 *Jiriki*, translated as "Self-Power," refers to the practitioner's attempt to achieve Enlightenment based on amassing personal merits. That is, to achieve the state of egolessness—to lose all

attachments to the false and temporary—through practice. This is contrasted with *Tariki*, or "Other-Power." Other-Power refers to the receiving of the (Amida) Buddha's Wisdom and Compassion and through this transformative power of the Buddha to participate in the formless truth.

36 The Recompensed Land refers to the Buddha Land that is formed after completing practices that fulfill vows that were established during the causal state (Bodhisattva) of the Buddha. It is called a Recompensed Land because the land that is established is in compensation for the practice that was completed to fulfill the Buddha's vows. In this particular passage, the Recompensed Land is referred to as "real" in contrast to the Provisional Recompensed Land. The Provisional Recompensed Land, or *Kedo*, is the land established for those multitudinous beings that are not able to free their minds of doubt and therefore cannot rely exclusively on the merit transference of Amida Buddha's Other-Power.

37 The same passage is translated in the *Collected Works of Shinran* as (page 462):
*'I fear it is hard to be born there by doing sundry good acts according to our diverse conditions.*
*According to our diverse conditions* refers to directing the merit of practicing various good acts, which one performs according one's own particular circumstances and opportunities, toward birth in the land of bliss. There are 84,000 gates of dharma. Since they are all good practices done in self-power, they are rejected as not leading to birth in the true fulfilled land. Thus, *I fear it is hard to be born.*"

38 The term "Easy Practice" was first introduced by Nagarjuna Bodhisattva in describing the Nembutsu path. In the *Igyobon* (lit. "Section on the Easy Practice") of the *Jujubibasharon* ("Treatise on the Explication of the Ten Stages") is written: "Within the Buddha-Dharma there are immeasurable gates. It is as it is with the world's paths. There is the difficult and the easy: the practice of walking over the (path) ways of the land is, in other words, arduous; riding the boat (over) water ways is, in other words, pleasurable. The path of the Bodhisattva is again this way: whether it is the effort of labored practice, or whether it is holding the expedient easy practice of faith."

39 Honen Shonin is the teacher of Shinran Shonin. Although Shinran Shonin uses the character *Hijiri* ("sage," or "master") for *Shonin*—meaning Master Honen—the Jodo Shinshu tradition has reserved this character to refer to Shinran Shonin. In referring to Honen

Shonin the character *Ue* ("superior") is used in the honorific term used for Honen Shonin.
40 This passage is found in Chapter 3 of the *Senjakuhongannembutsu-shu* where Honen Shonin talks about the meaning of the Primal Vow of Amida Buddha.
41 See also Section Four.
42 Prince Siddhartha would later in life become Shakamuni Buddha.
43 "Turning the Wheel of the Dharma," is an expression used to describe the Buddha sharing the contents of his Enlightenment experience with others. The image follows one of the Newtonian laws of motion (inertia) or "Once an object is put into motion it will stay in motion until an equal and opposite force acts upon it."

**Section Six**
44 The *Three Thousand Great Thousand Worlds* is comprised of incrementally larger "galaxies" that make up the Buddhist cosmos. The first of the *Three Thousand Great Worlds* is called a *"Small Thousand World."* A "World" is a complete system by itself and is comprised of many different elements. A thousand of these Worlds is what a *Small Thousand World* is comprised of. The next Thousand World is called a *"Medium Thousand World."* One *Medium Thousand World* is comprised of a thousand *Small Thousand Worlds*. Finally, the largest "galaxy" is called a *"Great Thousand World."* A *Great Thousand World* is comprised of a thousand *Medium Thousand Worlds*. Because there are three different types of Thousand Worlds (galaxies) it is collectively called the *Three Thousand Great Thousand Worlds*. It is an expression used to describe the expanse and totality of the Universe.
45 Having opposable digits, or the ability to touch our fingers with other fingers (our thumbs can touch all of our other fingers), gave human beings a distinct advantage in manipulating and holding very small objects.

**Section Seven**
46 The river is officially called the Ganga River. Internationally, however, it is known more by its Anglicized name or the Ganges.
47 The Bay of Bengal is a delta that is approximately 200 miles (320 km) wide.
48 The Ganges River's length is about 1,560 miles (2,510 km).

## Section Eight
49 See also Avaivartika found in Section Five.
50 See footnotes 16 and 22.
51 Faith in the Buddhist sense is not limited to "belief." For example, in describing the faith of the Primal Vow three separate qualities are described. The first can be described as the true and real heart that is filled with the Wisdom of the Buddha. The second is the faith of joy that comes from receiving the heart that is filled with truth. The third aspect, using the description above, can be described as the desire to become a full participant of the truth.
52 In the *Ichinen-tanen-mon-i* ("Meaning on Passages of One-Thought [versus] Many-Thoughts"), written by Shinran Shonin, is the passage, "this Sutra is called the *mumon jisetsu kyo* (lit. "Sutra without question that was explained by [Shakamuni Buddha] himself"). In explaining this Sutra, there was no one who gave a question to the *Tathagata*. This was understood to reveal the lesson that Shakamuni Buddha most wanted to share or in other words the reason for his appearance in this world. Because of this the Amida-kyo also came to be known as "The Sutra without question that was explained by [Shakamuni Buddha] himself."
53 Ashura is one of the six realms of existence. The Ashura is a warrior existence and one that characteristically cannot find pleasure without combat. See also footnotes 13 and 24

## People of the Amida-kyo
54 The other Bodhisattva that accompanies Shakamuni Buddha is Samantabhadra Bodhisattva (Jpz. *Fugen Bosatsu*)

# ABOUT THE AUTHOR

John Iwohara has been a Jodo Shinshu priest since 1983. After completing his graduate studies in Jodo Shinshu at Ryukoku University (Kyoto, Japan) in 1994 he has served at the temples in Fresno, California; Vista, California; Seattle, Washington and is currently at the Venice Hongwanji in Venice, California.

www.ingramcontent.com/pod-product-compliance
Lightning Source LLC
Chambersburg PA
CBHW051703090426
42736CB00013B/2518